W9-BDM-872

The iPod & iTunes PocketGuide

Christopher**Breen**

All the Secrets of the iPod, Pocket Sized.

**Peachpit
Press**

The iPod & iTunes Pocket Guide

Christopher Breen

Peachpit Press
1249 Eighth Street
Berkeley, CA 94710
510/524-2178
800/283-9444
510/524-2221 (fax)

Find us on the Web at: www.peachpit.com
To report errors, please send a note to errata@peachpit.com

Peachpit is a division of Pearson Education

Project editor: Kathy Simpson
Production editors: Myrna Vladic and Kate Reber
Compositor: Jerry Ballew
Indexer: James Minkin
Cover design: Aren Howell
Cover photography: Peachpit Press
Interior design: Kim Scott, with Maureen Forys
Additional support: Andrei Pasternak and Debbie Roberti

Notice of Rights

Notice of Liability

Trademarks

ISBN 0-321-40968-X

9 8 7 6 5 4 3 2

Printed and bound in the United States of America

Dedication

To my own little iBreen, Addie.

Acknowledgments

This book wouldn't be in your hands if not for the hard work and care of the following individuals.

At Peachpit Press: Cliff Colby (who edited a fair chunk of the first edition of the big ol' *Secrets of the iPod and iTunes* and proffered the original idea for an iPod book); Kathy Simpson (who copyedited every version of the big book and stepped in as editor of this guide to whisk it out the door with nary a glitch or bump); Rebecca Ross (who handled the contract negotiations with such aplomb); the three Nancys (Peterson, who edited the previous five editions of *SotiPaiT*; Davis, who Gives Final Approval; and Ruenzel, who makes everything go 'round); Myrna Vladic and Kate Reber (who coordinated production of the book); Scott Cowlin (who is a book-selling machine); Jerry Ballew (who laid out the book's pages), Andrei Pasternak and Debbie Roberti (who created some new illustrations and fixed some other ones), and James Minkin (who provided the index).

At home: My wife, Claire, who once again kept the other parts of our lives together while I applied nose to grindstone in the basement; and the boys of System 9 for being such groovy cats.

Abroad: Rick LePage and Jason Snell at *Macworld*, who, one fateful day, harmonized, "So, ya like iPods, eh? Howzabout we pay you to do nothing but write about them for a year?"

And, of course, the designers behind the iPod and iTunes. They just get better and better!

Getting Started

While I admire your desire to learn more about your iPod by purchasing this little guide, my guess is that before you delve too deeply into this book, you'd like to actually use your iPod. That's what this chapter is for—getting you up and running as quickly as possible. Here are the steps to take:

1. OPEN THE BOX.

After you've ripped the wrapping off your iPod, try turning it on. If it recently came from the factory, it could be charged and nearly ready to play.

To switch on any iPod except the iPod shuffle, press and hold the bottom of the wheel where you see the triangle and two parallel lines. If the iPod is charged, it should display an Apple logo after a few seconds and then be ready to roll in about

30 seconds. If nothing happens when you try to start the iPod, make sure that the Hold switch on the top isn't on. If you see any orange next to the switch, it means the Hold switch is on. Slide the switch over to disengage it. If the iPod still won't start, it must be charged.

For the iPod shuffle, flip it over and press the small rectangular button on the back. If a green light shows, the iPod is charged enough for you to play with it. If no light shows, it needs charging.

2. CHARGE IT (IF NECESSARY).

If the iPod doesn't work out of the box, you need to charge it up. On an iPod with a display (any iPod except the iPod shuffle), you can do this by plugging the included USB cable into your computer's powered USB 2.0 port and plugging the skinny end of the cable into the bottom of the iPod. If you have a charger for your iPod, you can also plug the USB cable into the charger, the skinny end of the cable into your iPod, and the charger into a wall socket.

The iPod shuffle is charged from your computer's powered USB port. Plug it in to charge the iPod.

3. INSTALL ITUNES.

If you don't already have a current copy of iTunes on your computer, install it from the software CD that accompanies your iPod. Follow whatever onscreen directions are necessary to put iTunes and the iPod software on your Windows PC or Mac.

4. RIP A CD.

No, don't actually rip the disc in half. *Rip* in this
context mean to record the audio from the CD
onto your computer. To do this, insert the disc into
your computer's CD or DVD drive, launch iTunes
(if it doesn't launch automatically after you've
inserted the disc), select the CD in iTunes' Source
list, and click the Import button at the top of
the iTunes window. The music on the CD will be
converted to a file format that can be played on
the iPod, and the tracks you ripped from the CD
will appear in iTunes when you click the Library
entry in the iTunes window.

5. PLUG IN THE IPOD.

If it's not plugged in already, plug your iPod into
your computer. With an iPod other than an iPod
shuffle, this means stringing the included USB cable
(or optional FireWire cable if you have a display-
bearing iPod other than a nano, which doesn't
support data transfer over FireWire) between the
appropriate port on the computer (USB 2.0 or
FireWire) and the Dock Connector port on the
bottom of the iPod. The iPod shuffle doesn't require
a cable; just plug it into a free USB 2.0 port.

If you're a Windows user, and this is the first time
you've connected a display-bearing iPod to your
computer, you'll be asked to run through a setup
assistant to format the iPod so that it works with
your computer. (iPod shuffles are already formatted
for Windows, so you won't have to jump through
any extra hoops with the shuffle.) Just follow along.

If you're a Mac user, a window will pop up, asking you to name your iPod. Feel free to accept or ignore Apple's invitation to register your iPod at this point.

If your computer is connected to the Internet via an always-on connection (DSL or cable broadband, for example), the iTunes Music Store window will open within the main iTunes window. Yes, Apple wants you to shop, but you don't have to.

6. TRANSFER MUSIC TO THE IPOD.

By default, the iPod is configured so that it auto-matically updates its music library when it's con-nected to your computer. The music you ripped from your CD should transfer quickly to the iPod. If it doesn't, simply choose Update Songs on *The Name of Your iPod* (where *The Name of Your iPod* is ... well, the name of your iPod) from iTunes' File menu.

7. UNMOUNT AND PLAY.

When the music has finished transferring, locate the name of your iPod in iTunes' Source list, and click the little Eject icon next to it. When the iPod disappears from iTunes, unplug it from your computer.

Unwrap the earbuds that came with the iPod, put a couple of those fuzzy covers over the earpieces and jam them into your ears, and plug the other end into the iPod's Headphone port. On an iPod with a display, rotate your thumb around the wheel on the front until Shuffle Songs is selected, and press the iPod's center button. On an iPod shuffle, just switch the iPod on by sliding the toggle switch on the back all the way down and then pressing the button on the front of the shuffle.

To adjust the volume on a click-wheel iPod, just rotate your thumb clockwise to increase volume and counterclockwise to turn it down. On a shuffle, press the + symbol on the top of the control ring to crank it up and the – symbol below to make it quieter.

8. ENJOY.

1

Meet the iPod

My guess is that you wouldn't be reading these words if an iPod weren't already part of your life—or soon to be part of your life. Congratulations. You've chosen to ally yourself with the world's most popular and—in my humble opinion—*finest* portable music player.

Oh, sure, there have been pretenders to the throne—countless "iPod killers" that, on closer examination, proved to be nothing more than less-capable and less-stylish wannabes. Despite multiple attempts to diminish its dominance, the iPod remains It—*the* music player to own.

And now that you do, it's time to become better acquainted with your musical buddy. To get started, let's take a tour through the various iPod models, and rummage around in the iPod's box.

Today's iPods

The danger of slapping a heading like "Today's iPods" in a book like this is that, given Apple's habit of revving the iPod line every six to nine months, Today's iPods may be Yesterday's iPods by the time you read this. However, unless the next-generation iPods breathe fire and project high-definition movies, the iPod you own shouldn't be disturbingly different from what I'm writing about in the autumn of 2005. Here's the lineup.

iPod

Figure 1.1 iPod

Photo courtesy of
Apple Computer

Throughout this little guide, I may refer to this iPod (**FIGURE 1.1**) as the *standard iPod* to differentiate it from the smaller iPod nano and iPod shuffle. To separate it from earlier monochrome standard iPods, I may also call it the *color iPod* or *iPod with color display.* I have to jump through these hoops because in midsummer 2005, Apple gave all its standard iPods color displays, and in September 2005, Apple replaced the monochrome iPod mini with the color iPod nano. Such displays were found only on a previous iPod photo model, which Apple discontinued when it bestowed color displays on all standard iPods, including the black-and-red iPod U2 Special Edition.

The iPod is offered in three configurations: the $299 20 GB iPod, the $399 60 GB iPod, and the $329 20 GB iPod U2 Special Edition. The 20 GB iPods hold around 5,000 four-minute songs encoded in AAC format at 128 Kbps (don't worry—I'll explain this whole encoding-and-Kbps thing in the chapters devoted to iTunes). The 60 GB iPod holds approximately 15,000 four-minute songs encoded in this same fashion. All of these iPods store music and data on an internal hard drive.

These iPods can not only play music, but also display pictures transferred from your computer or from a digital camera using a compatible transfer adapter. With the help of Apple's $19 iPod AV Cable, these iPods can display those pictures as slideshows on a connected television or digital projector. And unlike other iPod models, the standard iPod can record audio with the assistance of a compatible microphone attachment, such as Griffin Technology's $40 iTalk Voice Recorder or Belkin's $50 Voice Recorder for iPod w/Dock Connector.

Like all iPods, this model is powered by a rechargeable lithium-ion battery. Constant play time between charges on these iPods is around 15 hours if you don't muck too much with the iPod's controls and leave backlighting off. The battery will last through about five hours of constant use when you view pictures on the iPod's screen and about two hours when the iPod displays pictures on a connected television or through a projector. (In Chapter 7, I'll tell you how to get the greatest life out of that battery charge.)

Figure 1.2 iPod nano

Photo courtesy of Apple Computer

iPod nano

The iPod nano (**Figure 1.2**) is either black or white on the outside but colorful on the inside. Like the standard iPods, the sleek nano bears a crisp and colorful display (1.5 inches rather than 2 inches) and sports a click wheel for controlling the device. Also like its larger siblings, it has a Dock connector on the bottom; unlike those larger iPods, it has the Headphone port on the bottom too. The Hold switch remains on the top.

Apple offers the nano in two configurations: the $199 2 GB iPod nano and the $249 4 GB iPod nano. The first holds approximately 500 songs; the second holds twice as many (1,000 songs). Unlike the larger iPods, the iPod nano has no moving internal parts. Instead of being stored on a hard drive, music and data are stored on flash-media chips—solid-state storage circuitry that holds data. In addition to being tiny, these chips offer a singular advantage: They make playback skip-proof. Playback on a full-size iPod can skip if you're playing long or large tracks or if you bounce around a lot, as you might while exercising. This isn't an issue with the nano, as music is immediately fed from the flash chip to the nano's amplifier. This makes the nano an ideal workout companion. The iPod shuffle uses this same flash media.

Battery life on the nano is a little less than what you get on the color iPods. Apple claims approximately 14 hours of music play time and 4 hours of slideshow continuous play.

Although the nano supports picture viewing on the iPod, it won't project pictures to an attached television. Neither does it support voice recording or picture storage. And if you'd like to charge your nano from an external charger, you'll have to pay Apple $29 for the privilege, as a power adapter isn't included. Although the nano can be charged via either a FireWire or USB connection, it can sync only over USB.

iPod shuffle

This is Apple's "displayless iPod"—one that's about the size of a pack of gum and that includes no screen to indicate what the iPod is playing. Unlike the other iPods, the iPod shuffle (**Figure 1.3**) has no Dock Connector port but, rather, a male USB connector on the bottom that you plug into your computer's USB port to charge the iPod and transfer music and data. Although it has a controller in the shape of a wheel, the wheel doesn't spin; you simply press the wheel's outer ring to adjust volume and move from track to track (or to fast-forward or rewind through the currently playing track) and use the wheel's center button to play or pause the shuffle.

Figure 1.3
iPod shuffle

Photo courtesy of Apple Computer

The iPod shuffle can be had in a $99 512 MB config-uration or a $129 1 GB configuration, holding approx-imately 120 and 240 songs, respectively. As I mentioned earlier, the shuffle uses flash memory rather than a hard drive, which makes the shuffle another good choice for the gym.

This iPod also has a lithium-ion battery (though it's very, very small). Apple rates constant play time between charges at around 12 hours for the shuffle. In my tests, I got more than 17 hours of play time from a 512 MB shuffle under ideal conditions.

Given the shuffle's price and size, you can understand that it has certain limitations. The lack of a display is the most obvious one. This is not the iPod to own if you want to find and play a specific track easily. Instead, you should think of the iPod shuffle as your personal radio station—one that you've programmed with your favorite music so that you won't care which song it plays.

Because it lacks a display, there's no need for it to hold contacts, calendars, and notes—which other iPod models can display. Naturally, it won't hold pictures, nor will it record audio from an outside source. Also, it won't play tracks encoded in certain formats. It can play AAC, MP3, and WAV files, but it won't play AIFF and Apple Lossless files—the kind of large files that would quickly consume the shuffle's limited storage capacity. (I'll discuss encoders and formats when we visit iTunes in Chapter 3.) The shuffle is exactly what it appears to be: a basic music player.

Motorola ROKR phone

When is an iPod not an iPod? When it's a phone. Motorola's ROKR mobile phone (**Figure 1.4**) is the first of what will likely be a long line of phones that can play music downloaded from iTunes. As we go to press, the ROKR holds up to 100 tracks (music as well as podcasts) and is synced (*very* slowly) over the proprietary USB cable included with the phone.

Figure 1.4
Motorola's
ROKR phone

When you press the iTunes button on the face of the phone, you see an interface very much like what you see on an iPod (though the phone's interface is much slower than an iPod's). Unlike "real" iPods, the ROKR carries built-in stereo speakers (though you can also use it with headphones)..

The phone can play audio for about 15 hours on a single charge—which means you'll likely hear everything stored on it twice if you don't re-sync it with new material. The ROKR stores music on a removable 512 MB flash-media card.

Yesterday's iPods

I'd like to think that there are a lot of old iPods being passed from person to person as the original owners trade up. It's quite possible you have an older iPod, yet are new to this whole iPod business. This sidebar is for you. Here's how the various models shake out.

First-generation (1G iPod)

As the name implies, these are the very first iPod models. Originally released in late 2001 and early 2002, the first-generation iPod was offered in 5 and 10 GB configurations and bore a mechanical scroll wheel—a wheel, unlike the one on later iPods, that actually turned. Nothing on the back of an original 5 GB iPod indicates its storage capacity; the 10 GB model is marked as such on the back plate. These iPods support FireWire connections only and are incompatible with today's Dock-connector accessories. They also don't support playing files in the Apple Lossless format or recording audio from an external source.

Second-generation iPod (2G iPod)

The second white iPod came in 5, 10, and 20 GB capacities; sported a new, touch-sensitive scroll wheel; included redesigned earbuds that fit smaller ear canals more comfortably; and slapped a plastic cover over the FireWire port. This iPod bears the same limitations as the first-generation iPod in terms of support for Apple Lossless, Dock-connector accessories, and audio recording.

Third-generation iPod (3G iPod)

Whereas the second-generation iPods were an evolutionary release, these third-generation players were a redefinition of the original. The new iPods—available in capacities of 10, 15, 20, 30, and 40 GB— were sleeker and lighter. They featured a new front-panel design that placed touch-sensitive (and backlit) navigation buttons above the scroll wheel. Gone was the FireWire connector at the top of the iPod, replaced by a proprietary connector at the bottom of the unit

continues on next page

that supported both FireWire and USB 2.0 connections. (Charging over USB is not supported on these iPods, however.) A new remote connector was also added to the top of the 3G iPod. This connector was ostensibly for connecting Apple's Remote Control to the player, but it was later used by other accessories, such as Griffin Technology's iTrip FM transmitter and Belkin's iPod Voice Recorder.

iPod mini (1G and 2G mini)

Apple released a smaller version of the iPod in January 2004: the iPod mini. The first generation of minis were available in five colors—gold, silver, blue, green, and pink—the original mini was the first iPod to hold a 4 GB hard drive (called a *microdrive*), as well as the first iPod to sport a click wheel. The 2G minis came in brighter shades of blue, green, and pink (gold was discontinued, and the silver model looked the same as the 1G version), and were offered in 4 GB and 6 GB configurations. The mini was discontinued with the introduction of the iPod nano.

Fourth-generation iPod (4G iPod)

When Apple announced the fourth-generation iPod on July 19, 2004, it could have done so by proclaiming that the "maxi-mini" was born, for the fourth-generation iPod was, in some ways, closer in design to the iPod mini than to the previous three generations of white iPods. Available in 20 and 40 GB configurations, the fourth-generation iPod bore the same kind of click-wheel controller used on the mini. And like the mini, it could be charged via USB 2.0.

Apple iPod + HP, Apple iPod mini + HP, Apple iPod shuffle + HP

At one time, Hewlett-Packard sold iPods. No longer. These iPods were unique because . . . well, because they were sold by HP. Other than that, they were functionally identical to Apple's iPods. The only real difference between an hPod and an iPod was the warranty that covered the devices. HP's warranty was a bit more generous in terms of when you'd have to begin paying

continues on next page

to have your iPod fixed. HP canceled its iPod partnership with Apple in the summer of 2005.

iPod U2 Special Edition (monochrome version)

Though functionally no different from a 20 GB monochrome fourth-generation iPod, this special player was the first "big" iPod to come in colors—specifically, a black face with a red click wheel. Along with a coupon for $50 off U2's entire 400-plus song catalog from Apple's iTunes Music Store (normally priced at $149), this special iPod also carries the signatures of the four U2 members etched on the back plate. Like the standard 4G iPod, this model has been updated to include a color screen.

iPod photo

You can think of the iPod photo as either a 4G iPod with color and photo capabilities or as the current color iPod with *photo* appended to its name. This iPod—available in capacities of 30, 40, and 60 GB—existed as the higher-priced alternative to the monochrome 4G iPod. In addition to putting a bright and color-ful face on the now-dull-in-comparison 4G iPod, the iPod photo allowed you to view pictures and slideshows on your iPod (up to 25,000 pictures on the 60 GB model), as well as to project those pictures on an attached television or compatible projector.

Thinking inside the Box (Dock-Connector iPods)

At one time, Apple stuffed the iPod box with loads of goodies: in-ear headphones; a couple of cables for transferring data between your computer and iPod; a power adapter; a Dock and case for more-expensive iPods; a belt clip for the iPod mini; a video cable for iPods with color screens; a software CD and documentation; and, of course, the iPod itself. Rummage around in the box of an iPod you've purchased in the past couple of months, and you'll find that a lot of these items are now missing and available only as $19 or $29 add-ons.

No worries—what is in the box provides you enough to get started. Here's what you'll find inside the iPod and iPod nano boxes.

Earbuds

Your iPod comes with a set of headphones that you place inside—rather than over—your ears (**FIGURE 1.5**). This style of headphones is known as *earbuds*. Two foam disks fit over the earbuds. Apple includes two pairs of these foam disks in the box. These disks not only grip the inside of the ear—helping keep the earbuds in place—but also make the earbuds more comfortable to wear. (The hard plastic surface of the earbuds will begin to hurt after a while.) And yes, the disks clearly display detritus picked up inside your ears—thus discouraging others from borrowing your headphones.

Figure 1.5 The iPod's earbuds and pads

Just as you'll find a wide range of foot and head sizes among groups of people, the size of the opening to the ear varies. The earbuds included with the first generation of iPods were a little larger than other earbuds you may have seen. Some people (including your humble author) found these headphones uncomfortable. The latest iPods include smaller earbuds that I find much more comfortable. With the foam disks in place, you shouldn't have trouble keeping the earbuds in place, regardless of how large or small the openings to your ears are. But if you find the earbuds uncomfortable, you can purchase smaller or larger earbuds, or you can opt for a pair of over-the-ear headphones.

If the included earbuds do fit you, you may or may not be pleased with their performance. Apple made great efforts to create the finest music player on the planet, and it didn't skimp on the headphones, but sound is subjective, and you may find that other headphones deliver a more pleasing sound to your ears. If you believe you deserve better sound than your Apple earbuds provide, by all means audition other headphones.

USB 2.0 cable

The iPod's proprietary Dock connector (that thin port on the bottom of the iPod) is the avenue for both transferring music and information on and off the iPod and powering the device. The USB 2.0 cable included with the iPod can likewise perform double duty. When you string the cable between your iPod and your computer's powered USB 2.0 port, power flows through the cable and charges the iPod's battery. At the same time, this connection allows you to swap data—in the form of music and other files—between the player and computer.

The USB cable can also be attached to Apple's iPod USB Power Adapter (which is included with the iPod but not with the iPod nano and iPod shuffle) to charge the iPod's battery when it's not connected to a computer.

note The full-size iPod can use a FireWire 400 connection in the same way (the nano can charge, but not transfer data, only over FireWire). Indeed, the first iPods used *only* FireWire connections. As the iPod (and USB standard) matured, Apple opted to include USB cables only, though FireWire cables are still available as a $19 option.

As the iPod shuffle already comes with a USB connector, a USB cable is unnecessary.

Power adapter (iPod only)

As I said earlier, those who purchase a standard iPod (the white iPod or black U2 model) will find a power adapter in the box. Everyone else will either have to make do with charging the iPod through a computer's powered USB port or pungle up $29 to purchase Apple's power adapter (**Figure 1.6**).

Figure 1.6
Apple's USB
power adapter

tip Rather than make you wait until I discuss accessories later in the book, let me say right here and now that I believe purchasing a power adapter is a good plan. There will be times when it's inconvenient to charge your iPod from a computer—when you've plugged your iPod into your home stereo, for example, or your computer's USB ports are occupied by plugs from even-more-necessary computer peripherals. Having a power adapter gives you a lot more flexibility.

iPod Dock Adapter (iPod nano only)

This adapter looks similar to the Dock cradle adapters included with some iPod accessories. To assist iPod accessory manufacturers, which are forced to come up with a new cradle design every time Apple issues a new iPod, Apple has created a single one-size-fits-all-with-the-right-Apple-adapter specification for companies that participate in the Made for iPod program. This is the first of these adapters. As this book goes to press, no such accessories exist, but they likely will by the time you read this chapter.

Lanyard and USB cap (iPod shuffle only)

Give the shuffle's size, it's an easy item to misplace. To help prevent that, Apple provides a nylon lanyard with a plastic cap that fits over the USB connector. It's a cool enough way to show off your shuffle, but hanging such a nice bit of bling around your neck in one of the shadier parts of town might not be such a hot idea.

When you don't care to wear your shuffle around your neck, yet still wish to protect its USB connector, use the shuffle's USB cap—a rounded hunk of plastic that you'll likely lose in the first few weeks you own the iPod. (And yes, lots of companies sell cool and colorful replacement caps.)

Software, guides, and documentation

It seems you can't buy something as simple as a toaster these days without also gaining mounds of accompanying documentation. Apple tries not to overload you with useless paperwork, but each iPod is packaged with its fair share of paper that you're unlikely to read.

Given that you own this book, you can skip nearly all of the paperwork that comes with your iPod (unless the fine print of licensing agreements helps you sleep at night). The small "How Do I Use This Thing?" cheat card that accompanies the shuffle is worth keeping close at hand for your first couple of days of shuffle ownership, and any troubleshooting information—although not as complete as what you'll read here—is helpful for getting out of the quick jam.

The CD bundled with your iPod contains Windows and Mac versions of Apple's iTunes software—the software necessary to move music onto your iPod—as well as the iPod Updater software you'll use to reformat the device should something go wrong. You can download the latest versions of iTunes and the iPod Updater for free from Apple's Web site, so don't feel like you need to lock this disc in your safe deposit box (though it contains some documentation that's not offered in paper form).

2

Controls
and Interface

The iPod has rightly been praised for its ease of use.
As with all its products, Apple strove to make the iPod
as intuitive as possible, placing a limited number of
controls and ports on the device and making moving
from one screen to another a logical progression. In
the following pages, I scrutinize each iPod's controls
and examine the screens that populate the display-
bearing iPods.

On the Face of It

On the front of your iPod and iPod nano, you'll find a display and set of navigation controls. The shuffle dispenses with the display and provides a simplified set of controls. On the first two generations (1G and 2G) of the iPod, these controls were arrayed around a central scroll wheel and were mechanical—meaning that they moved and activated switches underneath the buttons. On the third-generation (3G) iPods, these controls were placed above the scroll wheel and were touch-sensitive; they activated when they came into contact with your flesh but, allegedly, not when a nonfleshy object (such as the case) touched them.

The iPod mini, fourth-generation (4G) and later full-size iPods, and the iPod nano bear a click wheel that incorporates the navigation buttons. Unlike the first two generations of the iPod, on which the buttons are arrayed around the outside of the wheel, these buttons are part of the wheel itself (**FIGURE 2.1**). Their sensors sit beneath the wheel at the four compass points, and the scroll wheel sits upon a short spindle that allows it to rock in all directions. To activate one of the buttons, just press the wheel in the direction of that button.

Figu 2.1 iPod's click wheel

The iPod shuffle's navigation controls are based on this wheel idea but don't parrot it. The ring around the center button is far narrower than you'll find on the mama and papa iPods, and it provides somewhat different functionality. Because of the shuffle's lack of a display and different controls, I'll discuss it separately.

iPod and iPod nano display and controls

The displays and controls of the iPod and iPod nano have a lot in common—so much that it only makes sense to discuss them together. Here's how each is laid out.

The displays

Near the top of the standard iPod sits a 2-inch-diagonal, color liquid crystal display that can show up to 65,536 colors at a resolution of 220 by 176 pixels. As with the nano, you can turn on backlighting (switch on a light that makes the display easier to read in low-light situations) by holding down the Menu button at the top of the click wheel. With all display-bearing iPods using iPod Software 1.3 Updater or later, you can also switch on backlighting by choosing Backlight in the iPod's main screen.

Measured diagonally, the nano's color display is half an inch smaller than that of the standard iPod, yet it projects as much text as its larger sibling. It does this by using a different font from the one used on the standard iPod.

The controls

The iPod and iPod nano feature the six controls described in the following sections.

Play/Pause button

If you scan the surface of your iPod or iPod nano, you'll notice that it bears no recognizable On/Off switch.

That job is handled by the Play/Pause button—located at the bottom of the iPod control wheel on older iPods, in the third position in the row of buttons on 3G iPods, and at the bottom of the click wheel on today's standard iPods and iPod nanos. Just press this button to switch the iPod on, and hold it down for about 3 seconds to switch the iPod off. On color iPods (including the nano), pressing this button while viewing a photo album initiates a slideshow.

Previous/Rewind button

This button is located on the far-left side of the wheel on 1G, 2G, and click-wheel iPods. It's the far-left button on 3G iPods. Press this button once to go to the beginning of the currently playing song; press twice quickly in succession to move to the previous song in the playlist; hold it down to rewind through a song. When you rewind or fast-forward through a song, you move in small increments at first. As you continue to hold the button down, you move in larger increments.

On color iPods, the Previous/Rewind button also moves you back through a slideshow.

Next/Fast Forward button

Look to the far right on 1G, 2G, and click-wheel iPods; look to the rightmost button on 3G iPods. Press this button once to go to the next song in the playlist; hold it down to fast-forward through a song. When you rewind or fast-forward through a song, you move in small increments at first. As you continue to hold the button down, you move in larger increments.

On color iPods (including the nano), the Next/
Forward button advances you through a slideshow.

Menu button

Pressing the well-marked Menu button takes you back
through the interface the way you came. If you've
moved from the main iPod screen to the Browse
screen, for example, and you press the Menu button,
you'll move back to the main iPod screen. If you've
moved from the main iPod screen through the Playlist
screen to a particular song within a particular playlist, each time you press the Menu button, you'll move
back one screen.

Holding the Menu button down for about 2 seconds
turns backlighting on or off.

Scroll wheel

Inside the ring of buttons on 1G and 2G iPods, below
the bevy of buttons on 3G iPods, and marked with the
navigation controls on click-wheel iPods and iPod minis
is the scroll wheel. Moving your thumb clockwise
highlights items below the selected item; moving the
wheel counterclockwise highlights items above the
selected item. If a window is larger than the display,
moving the scroll wheel causes the window to scroll
up or down when the first or last item in the list is
highlighted.

You also use the scroll wheel to adjust volume and
move to a particular location in a song.

Select button

The bull's-eye of all iPods—the center button—selects a menu item. If the Settings menu item is selected, for example, pushing the Select button moves you to the Settings screen, where you can select additional settings.

When you press the Select button while a song is playing and the Play screen is visible, you move to another Play screen, where you can *scrub* (quickly navigate forward and back with the scroll wheel) your song. On 3G and 4G monochrome iPods and iPod minis, pressing this button twice while a song plays moves you to a rating screen, where you can assign a rating of one to five stars to the song that's playing (**FIGURE 2.2**).

Figure 2.2
Display-bearing iPods and the ROKR phone let you rate songs from one to five stars.

tip On color iPods, you may have to press Select a time or two more to get past the Album Artwork screen (and, in the case of the nano, the Lyrics screen) to reach the Ratings screen.

iPod shuffle status light and controls

There's no need to mention the shuffle's display, because it hasn't got one. It does have a status light that tells you what it's doing, however, as well as

navigation controls on the front and a power/
play-order switch on the back. Here's how they work.

Status light

Buried beneath the plastic at the top end of the
shuffle (the end with the Headphone port) are a
couple of small lights (LEDs). When you first turn a
charged shuffle on, a light glows green for about
3 seconds. When you press Play or any part of the
outer ring, the green light briefly appears again. If
you pause playback, the green light blinks for just
under a minute. When you lock the shuffle, an amber
status light blinks three times rapidly. Press any of
the controls while the shuffle is locked, and you'll see
this same amber glow.

When you plug the shuffle into a power source, its
amber light will glow continuously and then switch
to the green LED when the shuffle is fully charged.

Outer ring

The ring that surrounds the inner Play/Pause button
handles track "navigation" (such as it is) and volume
control (**Figure 2.3**). Press the top part of the ring
(marked with a +) to increase volume. Press the
bottom of the ring (marked with a –) to turn the
volume down. The right side of the ring controls
the iPod's Next/Fast Forward function; press once
to move to the next track, or press and hold to fast-
forward through the currently playing track.

Figure 2.3 iPod
shuffle's control
wheel

The Previous/Rewind button on the left side of the ring
works like the Previous/Rewind buttons on other

iPods. Press once, and the currently playing song starts at the beginning. Press twice quickly in succession to move to the previous song in the playlist.

Play/Pause button

Yes, the Play/Pause button does what it says. With the shuffle switched on, press the button once to play; press it again to pause.

Because the shuffle has so few controls, Apple has pressed this button into service to perform other jobs. To go to the beginning of a playlist, for example, press this button three times quickly (within a second). To lock the iPod (disable its buttons), press and hold the button for about 3 seconds. To unlock it, press and hold the button again.

note When you lock the shuffle, its status light blinks three times. When you unlock it, the light briefly glows green.

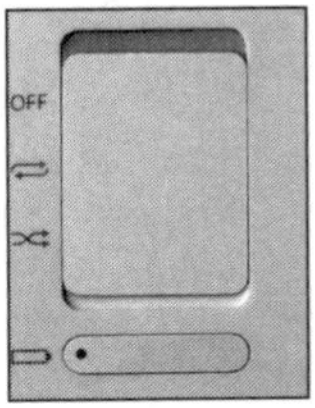

Figure 2.4 iPod shuffle's power switch and battery-power indicator

Power/play-order switch

The back of the shuffle has a three-position toggle switch (**FIGURE 2.4**). When the switch is pushed all the way to the top, the shuffle is off. Move the switch down one position, and the shuffle will play its playlist in order from beginning to end. Shift the switch all the way to the bottom position, and the iPod will live up to its name and shuffle its playlist randomly, playing all the songs on it before repeating any.

Battery-status button/light

Below the shuffle's switch is a rectangular button that, when pushed, gives you a very broad hint as to how much power is left in the shuffle. I say *broad* because it can glow green—which indicates a full charge—even after the shuffle has played for several hours. If you see an amber light, the shuffle is low on power. A red light indicates it's *really* low on power, and no light at all tells you that the shuffle is completely drained and should be plugged into a power source to charge.

Ports and connectors: Dock-connector iPods

The iPod doesn't work by osmosis. You need a hole for the sound to get out (and, in some cases, in) and another hole for moving data on and off the device. Here's what you'll find on the Dock-connector iPods.

Headphone jack and Hold switch

The 3G and all click-wheel iPods except the iPod nano sport a Headphone jack, a Hold switch, and a Remote Control connector up top (**Figure 2.5** and **Figure 2.6**). The Headphone jack and Hold switch work nearly the same way as they do on the older iPods, providing

Figure 2.5 *(left)*
Top of the 4G iPod

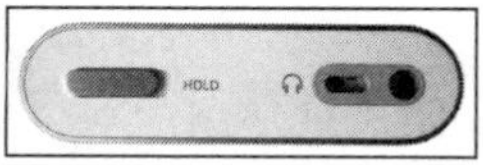

Figure 2.6 *(right)*
Port cap atop the iPod mini

audio output and disabling the iPod's controls. You'll find the iPod nano's Hold switch on top but the

Headphone port on the bottom (**Figure 2.7**). The nano has no Remote Control port.

Figure 2.7 Top of the iPod nano

tip

I say **NEARLY** because the Headphone jack, in combination with the Remote Control connector on 3G-and-later standard iPods, supports not only audio output, but also audio input. With a compatible microphone, you can record low-quality audio (8 kHz) on your iPod. See Chapter 6 for more on compatible iPod microphones.

note

The standard color iPod's Headphone jack is different from that on other iPods in that it's capable of also transmitting composite video. Though an iPod nano can display pictures on its screen, it doesn't support connections to external video devices.

Dock Connector port

On the bottom of the Dock-connector iPod, you'll find a proprietary port that handles both power and data chores for the device. This port, on the bottom of the 3G iPods and all click-wheel iPods save the iPod nano, supports data transfer via both FireWire and USB 2.0 (**Figure 2.8** and **Figure 2.9**). The nano can

Figure 2.8 Dock Connector port at the bottom of the iPod

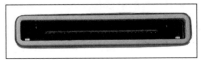

Figure 2.9 *(left)*
iPod mini's Dock
Connector port

Figure 2.10 *(right)*
iPod nano's
Headphone and
Dock Connector
ports

be charged via a FireWire connection but syncs only over USB (**Figure 2.10**).

Ports and connectors: iPod shuffle

The top of the iPod shuffle has exactly one hole: the Headphone port (**Figure 2.11**). Plug your earbuds or other headphones into this hole, switch on your shuffle, press Play, and enter the world of audio Nirvana (or Pearl Jam, if that's more your taste in grunge rock).

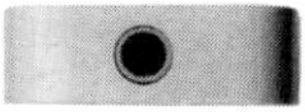

Figure 2.11
iPod shuffle's
Headphone port

Flip the shuffle over, pull off its protective cap, and spy the USB connector (**Figure 2.12**). Plug that into your computer's powered USB 2.0 port to charge the iPod and then transfer music and data to it.

Figure 2.12 USB
connector at the
bottom of the
iPod shuffle

Navigating the Screens

Considering how easy the iPod is to use, it's hard to believe the number of navigation screens that make up its interface. In the following pages, I scrutinize each screen. Except where indicated, the interfaces for the original iPod and the iPod nano are exactly the same.

Main screen

The main screen (**Figure 2.13**), which displays the word *iPod* at the top, is your gateway to the iPod. In a way, it's akin to the Mac's Finder or Windows' My Computer window—a place to get started.

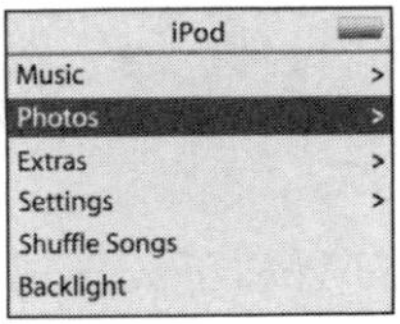

Figure 2.13 iPod's main screen

The color iPod's main screen contains these commands:

- Music
- Photos
- Extras
- Settings
- Shuffle Songs
- Backlight
- Now Playing (if a song is playing or paused)

By default the nano doesn't include the Backlight command in the Main screen. In the main screen on an iPod mini and an original monochrome iPod running iPod Software 1.3 Updater through iPod Software 3.1 Updater (the version of the iPod software current for fourth-generation (4G) iPods as this book goes to press), you can, by default, select the following items (**FIGURE 2.14**):

Figure 2.14 iPod mini's screen

- Music
- Extras
- Settings
- Shuffle Songs
- Backlight
- Now Playing (if a song is playing or paused)

Earlier versions of the iPod software do not include the Backlight command; instead, they offer an About command. On iPods running iPod Software 1.3 Updater or later, the About command is available in the Settings screen (described later in this chapter). Here's what you'll find within each item.

Music

When you choose the Music command and press Select, the resulting Music screen reveals these entries: Playlists, Artists, Albums, Songs, Podcasts (click-wheel iPods only), Genres, Composers, and Audiobooks (**Figure 2.15**). I explain the purpose of all these entries in the following sections.

Figure 2.15 iPod's Music screen

Playlists

Regardless of which iPod you're using, when you choose Playlists and press the Select button, you'll see a screen that contains the playlists you have downloaded to your iPod (**Figure 2.16**). These play-lists are created and configured in iTunes or another music application, such as the Windows programs Musicmatch Jukebox, EphPod, Anapod Explorer, and XPlay. How you configure them is up to you. You may, for example, want to gather all your jazz favorites in one playlist and put ska in another. Or, if you have an iPod shared by the family, Dad may gather his psychedelic songs of the '60s in his personal playlist, whereas sister Sue creates a playlist full of hip-hop and house music. When I discuss iTunes and other music applications in later chapters, I'll look at additional approaches for putting together playlists.

Figure 2.16
Playlists screen

II   Playlists   ▬
Beatles   >
Comes a Time   >
Get Back   >
Greensleeves   >
iTrip Stations   >
Jazz   >

note
You may notice a couple of other playlists that you didn't create: '90s Music, My Top Rated, Recently Added, Recently Played, and Top 25 Most Played, for example. These are Smart Playlists—playlists automatically created by iTunes. As their names hint, these playlists list songs recorded in the '90s, songs that you think are just swell, songs that you've just placed in iTunes, songs you've played in the not-too-distant past, and songs that you've played more often than others.

After you select a playlist and press the Select button, the songs within that playlist appear in a scrollable screen (**FIGURE 2.17**), and the name of the playlist appears at the top of the screen. Just select the song you want to play, and press the Select button. When you do, you'll move to the Now Playing screen (**FIGURE 2.18**), which can display the number of songs in the playlist; the name of the song playing; the artist; and, on the original iPod, the name of the album from which the song came.

Figure 2.17 *(left)*
Songs within a
playlist

Figure 2.18 *(right)*
Now Playing
screen

On a color iPod and iPod nano, you'll also see a picture
of the album cover if the song has this information
embedded in it and iTunes' Display Album Artwork
on Your iPod option is enabled. (Monochrome iPods
don't display album artwork.) Also appearing in
this screen are two timer displays: elapsed time
and remaining time. The screen contains a graphic
thermometer display that gives you a visual
representation of how far along you are in the song.

note

Text that runs off the screen in the Song, Artist, and Album
screens is treated differently on color iPods and the iPod
nano than it is on other iPods. Earlier white iPods and
the iPod mini place an ellipsis (...) at the end of an entry
that exceeds the width of the screen. A color-display
iPod will scroll selected text from right to left if it's
longer than the screen can accommodate.

You can move one more screen from the Now Playing
screen by using the scroll wheel or Select button.
If you turn the scroll wheel, you'll move to a screen
nearly identical to the Now Playing screen where you
can adjust the iPod's volume (**FIGURE 2.19**). When you
stop moving the scroll wheel, you'll be taken back to
the Now Playing screen after a couple of seconds. If
you press the Select button while you're in the Now
Playing screen, you'll be able to scrub through the song
(**FIGURE 2.20**).

Figure 2.19 *(left)* Now Playing screen's volume control

Figure 2.20 *(right)* Now Playing screen's scrub control

Like the Now Playing screen, the Scrub screen carries a thermometer display that indicates the playing location with a small diamond. Just push the scroll wheel back or forth to start scrubbing. The color iPod and iPod nano include one or two more screens after the scrub screen. On both of these iPods, if you have album artwork embedded in a track, pressing Select twice while in the Now Playing screen shows you a full-screen version of the album cover. If you've added lyrics to a track with iTunes 5, pressing Select three times from the Now Playing screen will take you to a Lyrics screen.

On-The-Go (Dock-connector iPods)

Scroll to the bottom of the Playlists screen on a 3G or Dock-connector iPod, and you'll find an additional playlist that you didn't create: the On-The-Go playlist (**Figure 2.21**).

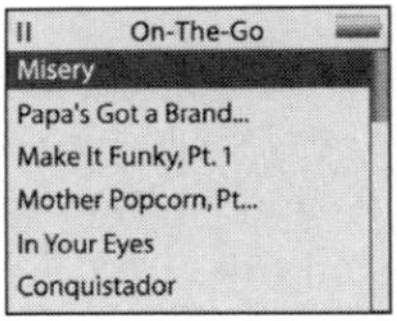

Figure 2.21 On-The-Go menu allows you to create custom playlists directly on the iPod.

Introduced with iPod Software 2.0 Updater, this playlist is a special one that you create directly on the iPod. It's particularly useful when you need to create a new playlist *right now* and don't have a computer you can plug your iPod into. It works this way:

1. Select a song, artist, playlist, or album.

2. Hold down the Select button until the selected item flashes a few times.

This flashing indicates that the item has been added to the On-The-Go playlist.

3. Repeat this procedure for any other songs, artists, playlists, and albums you want to add to the list.

4. When you're ready to play your selections, choose On-The-Go from the Playlists screen, and press the Select button.

In the resulting On-The-Go screen, you'll see a list of songs you've added to the list, in the order in which you added them. (The song, artist, playlist, or album you selected first will appear at the top of the list.)

5. Press Select to begin playing the playlist.

To clear the On-The-Go playlist, scroll to the bottom of the playlist, and select Clear Playlist. In the resulting Clear screen, select Clear Playlist; then press Select.

When you update a 3G iPod that's running the iPod Software 2.1 Updater or later, the On-The-Go playlist you created appears in iTunes' Source list as well as in the iPod's Playlist screen—thus ensuring that you don't lose the contents of the playlists you so carefully created on the iPod. Each such playlist is numbered successively: On-The-Go 1, On-The-Go 2, and On-The-Go 3, for example. These playlists are copied back to your iPod, and the On-The-Go entry is cleared.

On the click-wheel iPods running the latest iPod Software Updater, Apple expands the On-The-Go playlist's capabilities, allowing you to create multiple On-The-Go playlists on your iPod. To do so, follow these steps:

1. Follow the steps above to create an On-The-Go playlist.

2. Scroll to the On-The-Go entry in the Playlists screen, and press Select.

   The songs you added to your playlists appear in the On-The-Go screen.

3. Scroll to the bottom of the On-The-Go screen, select Save Playlist, and press Select.

4. In the resulting Save screen, scroll to Save Playlist, and press Select.

   Your playlist will be saved as New Playlist 1. Each time you save a new On-The-Go playlist, it will be called New Playlist and assigned a number one greater than the last New Playlist created.

When you synchronize your click-wheel iPod with iTunes, your saved On-The-Go playlists will appear successively numbered in iTunes, bearing the name On-The-Go—On-The-Go 1, On-The-Go 2, and (you guessed it) On-The-Go 3, for example. During synchro-nization, these On-The-Go playlists are copied to your iPod, and the New Playlist entries are removed.

Artists

The Artists screen displays the names of any artists on your iPod (**Figure 2.22**). Choose an artist's name and press Select, and you'll be transported to that artist's screen, where you have the opportunity to play every song on your iPod by that artist or select a particular album by that artist.

You'll also spy the All entry at the top of the Artists screen. Should you choose this entry, you'll be taken to the All Albums screen, where you can select all

Figure 2.22
Artists screen

albums by all artists. The All Albums screen contains an All command of its own. Select this command, and you'll move to the All Songs screen, which lists all songs by all artists on your iPod. (But if a song doesn't have an artist entry, the song won't appear in this screen.)

Albums

Choose the Albums entry and press Select, and you'll see every album on your iPod (**Figure 2.23**). Choose an album and press the Select button to play the album from beginning to end. The Albums screen also contains an All button, which, when selected, displays all the songs

Figure 2.23
Albums screen

on all the albums on your iPod. (If the song doesn't have an album entry, it won't appear in this screen.)

note An album entry can contain a single song. As long as the album field has been filled in for a particular song within iTunes or another iPod-compatible application (I'll discuss this topic in Chapter 3), that song will appear in the Albums screen.

Songs

Choose Songs and press Select, and you'll see a list of all the songs on your iPod (**Figure 2.24**).

Figure 2.24
Songs screen

Podcasts (click-wheel iPods only)

The click-wheel iPods next include a Podcasts entry (**Figure 2.25**). As you'll learn later in the book, *podcasts* are Internet broadcasts that you download and place on your iPod for later listening. Podcasts downloaded through the iTunes Music Store are routed to your iPod and placed under this entry on click-wheel iPods. On earlier iPods, you'll find the Podcasts entry in the Playlists screen.

Figure 2.25
Podcasts screen

Genres

The iPod has the capability to sort songs by genre: Acoustic, Blues, Reggae, and Techno, for example. If a song has been tagged with a genre entry, you can choose it by genre in the Genres screen (**Figure 2.26**).

Composers

The iPod can also group songs by composers. This feature, added in iPod Software 1.2 Updater, allows you to sort classical music more easily (**Figure 2.27**).

Figure 2.26 *(left)*
Genres screen

Figure 2.27 *(right)*
Composers
screen

II Genres	
Reggae	>
Rock	>
Soul	>
Soundtrack	>
Spoken Word	>
Techno	>

II Composers	
J.S. Bach	>
K. Stockhausen	>
Lennon	>
Lennon/McCartney	>
Little Willie John...	>
Luther Dixon	>

Audiobooks

The iPod is capable of playing audiobook files purchased from Audible.com and the iTunes Music Store. These audiobooks can be identified by their extension—.aa if you purchased the book from Audible.com or .m4b if you bought it from the iTunes Music Store. When an iPod stores one of these specially formatted files, the audiobook's name appears in the iPod's Audiobooks window (which appears when you choose the Audiobooks command in the Music screen and press the Select button).

Photos (color-display iPods only)

The Photo command appears only on iPods with color displays (**Figure 2.28**). This command is your avenue for configuring how slideshows are displayed on the iPod and, if you have a full-size color iPod, on an attached television or projector.

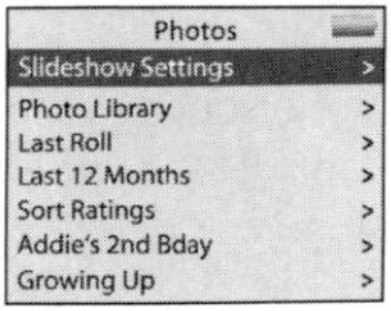

Figure 2.28
iPod's Photos
screen

Photos	
Slideshow Settings	>
Photo Library	>
Last Roll	>
Last 12 Months	>
Sort Ratings	>
Addie's 2nd Bday	>
Growing Up	>

Within the Photos screen, you'll find the following entries (except where noted).

Slideshow Settings

The Slideshow Settings screen contains a host of commands, described in the following sections.

Time Per Slide

You can configure the iPod so that slideshows are under manual command and you need to press the Next or Previous button to navigate the slideshow. You can also have the iPod change slides automatically every 2, 3, 5, 10, or 20 seconds.

Music

Your slideshow can be accompanied by music. From the Slideshow Music screen, choose iPhoto,

Now Playing, Off, one of the playlists on the iPod, or the On-The-Go playlist.

Repeat

If you like, you can have your slideshow repeat forever (or at least until the iPod runs out of power). This is a simple On or Off command.

Shuffle Photos

Another On and Off command. Off means that your slides play in order; choose On, and they're displayed randomly.

Transitions

The color iPods offer built-in *transitions* (effects that occur when you move from one slide to another). The included effects are Random (a random mix of effects), Push Across, Push Down, Wipe Across, Wipe Down, and Wipe from Center.

TV Out (full-size color iPods only)

This tells the iPod whether to output its video signal via the Headphone jack or the S-Video port on an attached color iPod's Dock. Off means no signal. Ask means that when you call up a photo library on the iPod and press Play to begin the show, a screen will appear, asking you if you'd like the TV signal turned on or left off. On means that the iPod will automatically send the signal out the Headphone jack.

tip   Turning on TV output depletes the battery charge in a big way—reducing slideshow play time from 5 hours to 2. Switch this option on only if you really need it.

TV Signal (full-size color iPods only)

The world has two major television standards: NTSC (United States and Japan) and PAL (Europe and Australia). You can choose either for your iPod's video output.

Photo Import (full-size color iPods only)

Full-size color iPods can import photos from a digital camera that uses Apple's $29 iPod Camera Connector and from Compact Flash cards plugged into the iPod via Belkin's $50 Media Reader for iPod w/Dock Connector. When you import photos with one of these devices, this command appears in the Photos screen. Click it, and you'll find a list of all the rolls (import sessions) you've brought into the iPod.

Photo Library

Press this entry to view all the photos stored on your iPod. Below the Photo Library entry, you'll find a list of all the photo albums that iTunes has imported onto your iPod. Select the album you want to view, and press Play to view the slideshow.

Extras

The Extras screen is the means to all the iPod's nonmusical functions—its contacts, calendars, clock, and games. Here's what you'll find for each entry.

Clock

Yes, the iPod can tell time. Clicking Clock displays the current time and date on all iPods. On 3G iPods and click-wheel iPods except the nano clicking Clock also displays commands for setting the iPod's alarm clock, sleep timer, and the date and time (**Figure 2.29**).

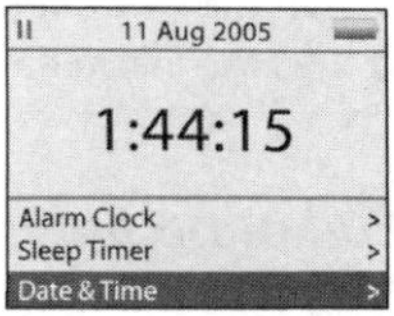

Figure 2.29
Clock screen

```
┌──────────────────────────┐
│ II      11 Aug 2005   ▭  │
│                          │
│       1:44:15            │
│                          │
│ Alarm Clock           >  │
│ Sleep Timer           >  │
│ Date & Time           >  │
└──────────────────────────┘
```

The iPod nano offers a different Clock screen—one that displays both an analog and digital clock in the top part of the screen and a New Clock entry at the bottom of the screen. Select New Clock and press Select to view the Region screen, where you view such regions as Africa, Asia, Europe, and North America. Select a region and press Select again, and choose a city in the resulting City screen.

When you select a clock on the nano and press Select, you'll see these settings for that clock: Alarm Clock, Change City, Daylight Saving Time, Delete This Clock, and Sleep Timer.

Alarm Clock

The Alarm Clock screen provides options for turning the alarm on and off, setting the time for the alarm to go off, and specifying the sound the alarm will play (a simple beep or the contents of one of the playlists on your iPod). This function is not available on 1G and 2G iPods.

tip
If the iPod's alarm clock goes off while you're listening to music with headphones, you're likely to miss the alarm if it's set to beep. Unlike alarms tied to calendar events, the alarm clock issues no visual display; it beeps or plays a playlist—that's it. If you think you'll be listening to music when the alarm is configured to perform its lowly job, choose a playlist as an alarm rather than a beep. When the iPod suddenly changes playlists, you'll know that the alarm has gone off.

Change City (iPod nano only)

Click this entry to be taken to the Region screen, where you can choose a new region and city for the clock.

Daylight Saving Time

This is a simple on/off command.

Delete This Clock

You know ...

Sleep Timer

To save battery power, the iPod includes a sleep function that powers down your iPod after a certain amount of time has elapsed. The Sleep Timer settings allow you to determine how long an interval of inactivity has to pass before your iPod takes a snooze. The available settings are Off, 15 Minutes, 30 Minutes, 60 Minutes, 90 Minutes, and 120 Minutes. On older iPods, this command is in the Settings screen.

Date & Time

The Date & Time command is your means for setting the time zone that your iPod inhabits, as well as the current date and time. On older iPods and the iPod nano, this command and its subcommands are accessed from the Settings screen.

Set Time Zone Click this command, and in the resulting Time Zone screen, choose your time zone—anything between and including Eniwetok to Auckland. This function is not available on 1G and 2G iPods.

Set Time & Date Select and click this command to set the iPod's date and time. Use the scroll wheel to change the hour, minutes, AM/PM, date, month, and year values, and use the Forward and Previous buttons to move from value to value. This function is not available on 1G and 2G iPods.

Time Use this command to display a 12- or 24-hour clock. This function is not available on 1G and 2G iPods.

Time in Title This command allows the iPod to display the time in the iPod's title bar. This function is not available on 1G and 2G iPods.

tip On 3G-and-later iPods, the Set Time Zone, Set Date & Time, Time, and Time in Title commands are also available in the Date & Time screen that's accessible from the Settings screen.

Contacts

I'll discuss how to create contacts elsewhere in the book. In the meantime, you need to know only that to access your contacts, you choose Contacts in the

Extras screen and press the Select button (**FIGURE 2.30**).
Scroll through your list of contacts and press Select
again to view the information within a contact. If a
contact contains more information than will fit in the
display, use the scroll wheel to scroll down the window.

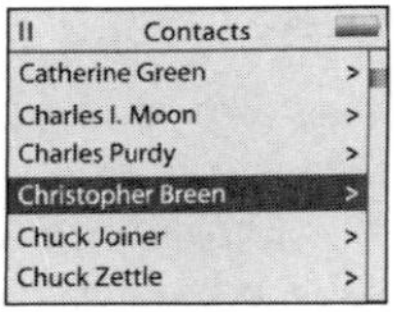

Figure 2.30
Contacts screen

If you haven't placed any contacts on your iPod, clicking
the Contacts command will reveal two entries in the
Contacts screen: Instructions and Sample. You can
probably guess that selecting Instructions provides
you directions on how to move contacts to your iPod.
The Sample command shows you what a complete
contact looks like.

Calendar

I'll also address calendar creation later in the book, so
for now, just know that when you click the Calendar
entry on a 3G iPod or click-wheel iPod, you'll see
options for viewing all your calendars in a single
calendar window, viewing separate calendars (your
work or home calendar, for example) if you've created
your calendars on the Mac with Apple's iCal, viewing
calendars you've created with applications other
than iCal under an "Other" heading, viewing To Do
items, and setting an alarm for calendar events.

When you select a calendar, the current month is displayed in a window with the current day highlighted

(**FIGURE 2.31**). If a day has an event attached to it, that day displays a small black rectangle. Use the scroll wheel to move to a different day; scroll forward to look into the future, and scroll back to be transported back in time. To jump to the next or previous month, use the Fast Forward or Back button, respectively. When you want to see the details of an event, scroll to its day and press the Select button. The details of that event will be displayed in the resulting screen.

Figure 2.31
Calendar screen

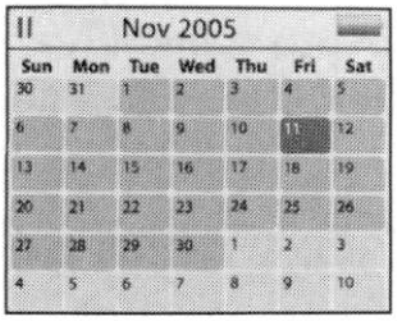

Older iPods have more limited calendar functions. Although you can view all your calendars, individual calendars created with iCal, and "Other" calendars created by applications other than iCal, you can't view To Do items. On these iPods, you configure calendar alarms in the Settings screen. The three available settings are Off (no alarm is issued), On (a little tinkling sound erupts from the iPod—the iPod itself, not the headphones—and an alarm screen that describes the event is displayed), and Silent (the alarm screen appears without audio accompaniment).

Calendar alarms for 3G iPods and click-wheel iPods appear in the Calendars screen. The three alarm options on these iPods are Off, Beep (the same thing as On for older iPods), and Silent.

Notes

New with the 3G iPods was a Notes feature that allows you to store text files (up to 4 KB, or about 4,096 characters) on your iPod. To add notes to your iPod, mount the iPod on your computer (the iPod must be configured to appear on the desktop), double-click the iPod to reveal its contents, and drag a text file into the iPod's Notes folder. When you unmount your iPod, you'll find the contents of your text file in the Notes area of the Extras screen. The 1G and 2G iPods don't have this function.

Voice Memos (3G, 4G, and full-size color iPods only)

Late-model standard iPods can record voice memos with a compatible microphone adapter. When you plug such an adapter into the Headphone jack and Remote Control port, the Voice Memos command appears in the iPod's Extras screen. Currently, only four devices—Belkin's Voice Recorder, Universal Microphone Adapter, and TuneTalk; and Griffin Technology's iTalk—are compatible with the iPod voice-recording function, and voice memos work only with 3G and 4G iPods and color iPods. (This feature is incompatible with the mini.)

Click the Select button, and you're taken to the Voice Memos screen, where you can choose to record a new voice memo or play back memos you've already recorded (**Figure 2.32**).

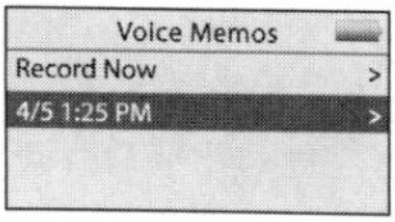

Figure 2.32 Voice
Memos screen

Stopwatch (iPod nano only)

The Stopwatch will track total time and lap time.
When you click Done to stop the watch, it saves your
times in a Stopwatch screen. Select one of these entries
and click the Select button, and you'll see a summary
that displays the date and time of the event; total time;
time for each lap; and such summary statistics as total
time, longest and shortest laps, and average lap time.

Screen Lock (iPod nano only)

Screen Lock is a feature for . . . well, locking your iPod's
screen. Like a cheap bike lock, this lock lets you create
a four-digit password using numbers from 0 through 9.
The interface features a round combination wheel
with four digits above it. To move from one digit to
another, use the Next and Previous buttons. Pressing
the Select button also takes you to the next digit and,
when you reach the final digit, sets the code. When
the nano is locked, you can pause and play it, but
nothing more; you can't adjust the volume, because
turning the wheel adjusts the selected digit. Even
when you reset the iPod, it boots back into the
Screen Lock screen.

Games

Once upon a time, the iPod had a single hidden
game that you could access only if you held down
the Select button for several seconds in a particular

screen. Apple later decided to reveal this secret game—a form of the classic Breakout game called Brick (**FIGURE 2.33**)—by placing the Game command in the Extras screen.

Figure 2.33 Brick game screen

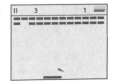

Apple includes three additional games—Music Quiz, Parachute, and Solitaire—with 3G iPods and click-wheel iPods. When you choose the Games option in the Extras screen of these iPods, you'll see listings for Brick, Music Quiz, Parachute, and Solitaire.

To play Brick, just select it and press the Select button. Press Select again to begin the game, and use the scroll wheel to move the paddle.

Music Quiz plays a random portion of a song stored on your iPod, which displays five titles on the iPod's screen (**FIGURE 2.34**). Your job is to scroll to the correct title and push the Select button as quickly as your fingers allow. The more swiftly you identify the song, the more points you earn. At the 7-second mark, one of the titles disappears; at 5 seconds, another vanishes, and so on until just one title remains and your time expires.

Figure 2.34 A Music Quiz screen

II 830
Lucy In The Sky With...
Five Guys Named Moe
I'm Looking Through...
Like a Rolling Stone
You Really Got A Hold...
Score: 0 10/111

In Parachute, your job is to rotate the cannon (using the scroll wheel) and blast helicopters and parachutists out of the sky. You lose the game when a certain number of parachutists lands safely or one parachuter lands directly on your cannon emplacement.

Solitaire is an implementation of the classic Klondike card game (**FIGURE 2.35**). To play, arrange alternating colors of cards in descending sequence—a sequence that could run jack of hearts, 10 of spades, 9 of diamonds, 8 of clubs, and so on—in the bottom portion of the screen. In the top portion of the window, you arrange cards in an ascending sequence of the same suit—ace, 2, 3, 4, and 5 of hearts, for example.

Figure 2.35
Yes, those little figures represent numbers and suits.

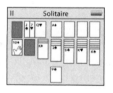

Navigating this game is not completely intuitive. Use the scroll wheel to move the hand pointer to the card you want to move. Press Select to move the selected card to the bottom of the screen. Then move the pointer to where you want to place the card, and press Select again. The game tries to be helpful by moving the pointer to the place where you're most likely to place the card.

Note: The Games entry is the second option in the iPod nano's Extras screen.

Settings

The Settings screen (**Figure 2.36**) is the path to your iPod preferences—including backlight timer and startup-volume settings, EQ selection, and the language the iPod displays. The following sections look at these settings individually.

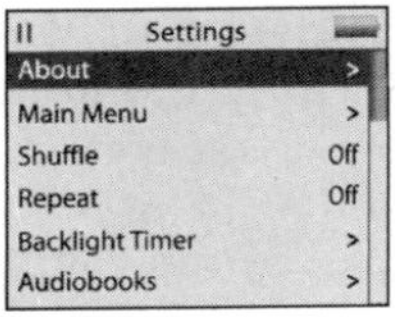

Figure 2.36
Settings screen

About

The About screen is where you'll find the name of your iPod (changeable within iTunes and such Windows players as Musicmatch Jukebox and XPlay), the number of songs the iPod currently holds (and, where applicable, the number of photos), the total hard-drive space, the amount of available space, the software version, and your iPod's serial number. If you have an iPod formatted for Windows, you'll also see the Format Windows entry. (The Mac version of the iPod doesn't bother to tell you that it's formatted for the Macintosh.)

Main Menu

The Main Menu command offers you a way to customize what you see in the iPod's main screen. Choose Main Menu, and press the Select button. In the resulting screen, you can choose to view a host of commands. To enable or disable a command, press the Select button to toggle the command on or off. To return the main menu to its default setting, choose the Reset Main Menu command, press Select, choose Reset in the Reset Menus screen, and press Select again.

Shuffle

Selecting Shuffle and pressing the Select button toggles you through three settings: Off, Songs, and Albums. On iPods without a click wheel, when Shuffle is set to Off, the iPod plays the songs in a playlist in the order in which they appear onscreen. The Songs setting plays all the songs within a selected playlist or album in random order. If no album or playlist is selected, the iPod plays all the songs on the iPod in random order. And the Albums setting plays the songs within each album in order but shuffles the order in which the albums are played.

Repeat

The Repeat setting also offers three options: Off, One, and All. When you choose Off, the iPod won't repeat songs. Choose One, and you'll hear the selected song play repeatedly. Choose All, and all the songs within the selected playlist or album will repeat when the playlist or album has played all the way through. If you haven't selected a playlist or album, all the songs on the iPod will repeat after they've played through.

Backlight Timer

The iPod's backlight pulls its power from the battery, and when it's left on for very long, you significantly shorten the time you can play your iPod on a single charge. For this reason, Apple includes a backlight timer that automatically switches off backlighting after a certain user-configurable interval. You set that interval by choosing the Backlight Timer setting.

On iPods prior to the color iPods, the settings available to you are Off, 2 Seconds, 5 Seconds, 10 Seconds, 20 Seconds, and (for those who give not a whit about battery life or who are running the iPod from the power adapter) Always On. Color iPods include one additional setting: 15 Seconds.

Audiobooks (click-wheel iPods only)

One of the unique features of the click-wheel iPods is their ability to slow down or speed up the playback of audiobooks without changing the pitch of the narrator. When you select Audiobooks in the Settings screen, you're offered three options in the resulting Audiobooks screen: Slower, Normal, and Faster. The Slower and Faster commands slow down or speed up playback by about 25 percent, respectively.

You're likely thinking that it would take a minor miracle to pull this off without making the book sound odd. You're right; it would. And so far, Apple has failed to achieve this miracle. When you slow down an audiobook, the resulting audio sounds like it was recorded in a particularly reverberant bathroom; you hear a very short echo after each word. Files that have been speeded up appear to have lost all the spaces between words, making the book sound as though it's being read by an overcaffeinated auctioneer.

EQ

EQ (or *equalization*) is the process of boosting or cutting certain frequencies in the audio spectrum—

making the low frequencies louder and the high frequencies quieter, for example. If you've ever adjusted the bass and treble controls on your home or car stereo, you get the idea.

The iPod comes with the same EQ settings as iTunes. Those settings include:

- Off
- Bass Booster
- Classical
- Deep
- Flat
- Jazz
- Loudness
- Piano
- R & B
- Small Speakers
- Treble Booster
- Vocal Booster
- Acoustic
- Bass Reducer
- Dance
- Electronic
- Hip Hop
- Latin
- Lounge
- Pop
- Rock
- Spoken Word
- Treble Reducer

Although you can listen to each EQ setting to get an idea of what it does, you may find it easier to open iTunes; choose Equalizer from the Window menu; and, in the resulting Equalizer window, choose the various EQ settings from the window's pop-up menu. The equalizer's 10-band sliders will show you which frequencies have been boosted and which have been cut. Any slider that appears above the 0 dB line indicates a frequency that has been boosted. Conversely, sliders that appear below 0 dB have been cut.

Sound Check

Sound Check attempts to maintain a consistent volume among all the songs on your iPod. Before Sound Check arrived on the scene, you'd constantly fiddle with the iPod's volume because one song was too loud, the next too quiet, the next quieter still, and the next painfully loud. Sound Check does its best to produce volumes that don't vary so wildly.

To use Sound Check, you must first enable the Sound Check option in the Audio pane of iTunes' Preferences window. iTunes will adjust the volume settings of the tracks in its Library, and when those tracks are transferred to your iPod, they will maintain the Sound Check settings imposed by iTunes.

Sound Check won't balance volumes on a per-album basis. This is a problem, because audio engineers intentionally make some songs softer than others—on ballads, for example. Sound Check ruins this loud/soft album-track relationship.

EQ and the iPod

Apple was kind enough to include a configurable equalizer (EQ) as part of the iPod Software 1.1 Updater and later, but the way that the EQ settings in iTunes and the iPod interact is a little confusing. Allow me to end that confusion.

Macintosh users undoubtedly know that in iTunes 2, 3, and 4, you can assign an EQ setting to songs individually by clicking the song, pressing Command-I, clicking the Options tab, and

continues on next page

then choosing an EQ setting from the Equalizer Preset menu. You can do the same thing in the Windows version of iTunes (EQ is not supported by Musicmatch Jukebox, however). When you move songs to your iPod, these EQ settings move right along with them, but you won't be able to use them unless you configure the iPod correctly.

If, for example, you have EQ switched off on the iPod, songs that have an assigned EQ preset won't play with that setting. Instead, your songs will play without the benefit of EQ. If you set the iPod's EQ to Flat, the EQ setting that you preset in iTunes will play on the iPod. If you select one of the other EQ settings on the iPod (Latin or Electronic, for example), songs without EQ presets assigned in iTunes will use the iPod EQ setting. Songs with EQ settings assigned in iTunes will use the iTunes setting.

If you'd like to hear how a particular song sounds on your iPod with a different EQ setting, start playing the song on the iPod, press the Menu button until you return to the Main screen, select Settings, select EQ, and then select one of the EQ settings. The song will immediately take on the EQ setting you've chosen, but this setting won't stick on subsequent playback. If you want to change the song's EQ more permanently, you must do so in iTunes.

Compilations (color iPods only)

Songs are usually given the compilations tag if they're part of a greatest-hits package or soundtrack album. Color iPods include a Compilations entry that lists all the albums with the compilations tag.

Sound Check

This option allows you to switch on or turn off iTunes' Sound Check option. (See Chapter 3 for details on Sound Check.)

Contrast (not available on color iPods)

To change the display's contrast, select the Contrast setting, press Select, and use the scroll wheel to darken or lighten the display.

Color iPods don't include any controls for changing the brightness, contrast, or color balance of the screen.

Clicker

When you choose Clicker on a click-wheel iPod and press the Select button, you have four options: Off, Speaker, Headphones, and Both. As the names imply, Speaker causes the iPod to emit a click sound from within the device; Headphones plays a click sound through the Headphone jack; and Both channels the click sound through both the internal speaker element and the Headphone jack.

Earlier iPods allow you only to turn the clicker on and off.

Date & Time

On 3G iPods and all click-wheel iPods except the iPod nano, this command is also accessible from the Date & Time command in the Clock screen.

As I said when discussing the Clock command, this command includes options for configuring the time zone, date, and time; displaying a 12- or 24-hour clock; and placing the current time in the iPod's title bar.

On 1G and 2G iPods, you can use this command to set only the time zone and the current date and time.

Contacts

The Contacts setting allows you to sort your contacts by last or first name and to display those contacts by last or first name.

Language

All iPods except the iPod nano can display 14 languages: English, Japanese, French, German, Spanish, Italian, Danish, Dutch, Norwegian, Swedish, Finnish, Korean, and Chinese (Traditional and Simplified). The nano displays seven additional languages.

Legal

If you care to view a few copyright notices, feel free to choose the Legal setting and press the Select button.

Reset All Settings

As the name implies, selecting Reset All Settings, pressing the Select button, and selecting Reset returns the iPod to its default settings. Your iPod's music will stay right where it is; this command just restores the interface to the way it was when the iPod came out of the box.

Shuffle Songs

One might think that choosing this option causes the iPod to play all the material on the iPod in random order. Not exactly. Shuffle Songs changes its behavior based on the Shuffle setting in the iPod's Settings screen. It works this way:

If you press Shuffle Songs when Shuffle is set to Off or to Songs, the iPod will play songs at random. (Note that it won't play any files it recognizes as audiobooks.)

If you press Shuffle Songs when Shuffle is set to Albums, the iPod picks an album at random and then plays the songs on that album in succession (the order in which they appear on the album). When that album finishes playing, the iPod plays a different album.

Note that if you also switch the Repeat command in the Settings menu to All and press Shuffle Songs, the iPod plays through all the songs on the iPod in the order determined by the Shuffle command and then repeats them in the same order in which they were shuffled originally. If you have three songs on your iPod—A, B, and C—and the iPod shuffles them to be in B, C, A order, when they repeat, they'll repeat as B, C, and A. The iPod won't reshuffle them.

3

iTunes and You

A high-performance automobile is little more than an interesting amalgam of metal and plastic if it's missing tires and fuel. Sure, given the proper slope (and, perhaps, a helpful tailwind), that car is capable of movement, but the resulting journey leaves much to be desired. So, too, the iPod is a less-capable music-making vehicle without Apple's music player/encoder, iTunes. The two—like coffee and cream, dill and pickle, and Fred and Ginger—were simply meant for each other.

To best understand what makes the iPod's world turn, you must be familiar with how it and iTunes work together to move music (and pictures, in the case of color iPods) on and off your iPod. In the following pages, you'll learn just that.

Ripping a CD

Apple intended the process of converting the music on an audio CD to computer data to be painless, and it is. Here's how to go about it:

1. Launch iTunes.

2. Insert an audio CD into your computer's CD or DVD drive.

Figure 3.1 This album's song tracks were downloaded from the Web automatically by iTunes.

By default, iTunes will try to identify the CD you've inserted and log on to the Web to download the CD's song tracks—a very handy feature for those who find typing such minutia to be tedious. The CD appears in iTunes' Source list, and the tracks appear in the Song list to the right (**FIGURE 3.1**).

3. To convert the audio tracks to a format compatible with your iPod—AAC, MP3, Apple Lossless, AIFF, or WAV—click the Import CD button in the top-right corner of the iTunes window.

(To import only certain songs, choose Edit > Select None and then click the boxes next to the songs you want to import. Click the Import CD button to import just those selected songs.)

iTunes begins encoding the files via the encoder chosen in the Importing tab of the Advanced pane of the iTunes Preferences window (**Figure 3.2**). By default, iTunes imports songs in AAC format.

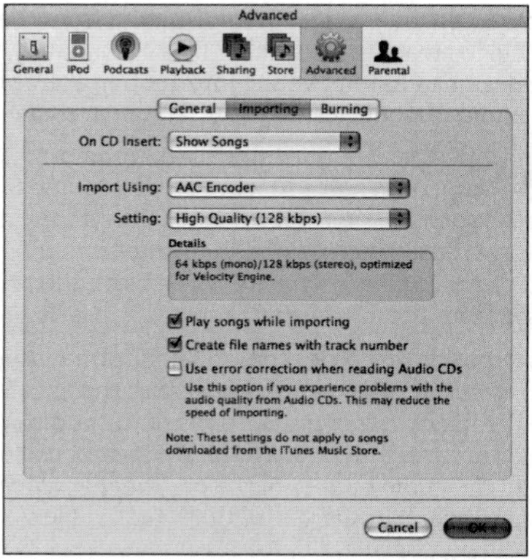

Figure 3.2
iTunes' default
file-encoding
settings

4. Click the Library button.

You'll see the songs you just imported.

5. To listen to a song, click its name in the list and then click the Play button or press the spacebar.

Import Business: File Formats and Bit Rates

MP3, AAC, AIFF, WAV . . . is the computer industry incapable of speaking plain English!?

It may seem so, given the plethora of acronyms floating through modern-day Technotopia. But the lingo and the basics behind it aren't terribly difficult to understand.

MP3, AAC, AIFF, and WAV are audio file formats. The compression methods used to create MP3 and AAC files are termed *lossy* because the encoder removes information from the original sound file to create these smaller files. Fortunately, these encoders are designed to remove the information you're least likely to miss—audio frequencies that you can't hear easily, for example.

AIFF and WAV files are uncompressed, containing all the data from the original. When a Macintosh pulls audio from an audio CD, it does so in AIFF format, which is the native uncompressed audio format used by Apple's QuickTime technology. WAV is a variant of AIFF and is used extensively with the Windows operating system.

iTunes supports one other compression format: Apple Lossless. This is termed a *lossless* encoder because the encoder doesn't shrink the file by removing portions of the audio spectrum; rather, it removes redundant data. This scheme allows you to retain all the audio quality of the original file while producing a copy just over half the size of that original file.

Now that you're familiar with these file formats, let's touch on resolution.

You probably know that the more pixels per inch a digital photograph has, the crisper the image (and the larger the file). Resolution applies to audio as well. But audio defines resolution by the number of kilobytes per second (Kbps) contained in an audio file. *With files encoded similarly,* the higher the kilobyte count, the better-sounding the file (and the larger the file).

continues on next page

I emphasize "with files encoded similarly" because the quality of the file depends a great deal on the encoder used to compress it. Many people claim that if you encode a file at 128 Kbps in both the MP3 and AAC formats, the AAC file will sound better.

The Import Using pop-up menu lets you choose to import files in AAC, AIFF, Apple Lossless, MP3, or WAV format. All display-bearing iPods can play files encoded in the AAC, MP3, AIFF, and WAV formats. Only Dock connector iPods can play songs formatted with the Apple Lossless Encoder. The iPod shuffle can play all these formats except AIFF and Apple Lossless.

The Configuration pop-up menu is where you choose the resolution of the AAC and MP3 files encoded by iTunes. iTunes' default setting is High Quality (128 Kbps). To change this setting, choose Custom from the Setting pop-up menu, and in the resulting AAC Encoder window, choose a different setting—in a range from 16 to 320 Kbps—from the Stereo Bit Rate pop-up menu (**Figure 3.3**). Files encoded at a high bit rate sound better than those encoded at a low bit rate (such as 96 Kbps). But files encoded at higher bit rates also take up more space on your hard drive and iPod.

The default settings for MP3 importing include Good Quality (128 Kbps), High Quality (160 Kbps), and Higher Quality (192 Kbps). If you don't care to use one of these settings, choose Custom from this same pop-up menu. In the MP3 Encoder dialog box that appears, you have the option to choose a bit rate ranging from 8 to 320 Kbps.

Figure 3.3
AAC encoding
options

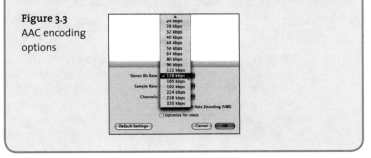

Moving Music into iTunes

Ripping CDs isn't the only way to put music files on your computer. Suppose that you've downloaded some audio files from the Web and want to put them in iTunes. You have three ways to do that:

- In iTunes, choose File > Add to Library.

  When you choose this command, the Add To Library window appears. Navigate to the file, folder, or volume you want to add to iTunes, and click Open (**FIGURE 3.4**). iTunes decides which files it thinks it can play and adds them to the Library.

Figure 3.4 The Add To Library navigation window

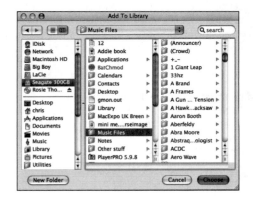

- Drag files, folders, or entire volumes to the iTunes icon in Mac OS X's Dock, the iTunes icon in Windows' Start menu (if you've pinned iTunes to this menu), or the iTunes icon in either operating system (at which point iTunes launches and adds the dragged files to the Library).

- Drag files, folders, or entire volumes into iTunes' main window.

In the Mac versions of iTunes, you'll find songs in the iTunes Music folder within the iTunes folder inside the Music folder inside your OS X user folder. So, for example, the path to my iTunes music files would be chris/Music/iTunes/iTunes Music.

Windows users will find their iTunes Music folder by following this path: *yourusername*/My Music/ iTunes/iTunes Music.

Copy Restrictions

The iPod was designed to be a one-way copying device: You can move music from your computer to your iPod, but you can't move music from the iPod to the computer. Apple designed the iPod this way to discourage music piracy.

For this same reason, the iPod is tied to one computer. When you plug your iPod into a computer other than the one it was origi-nally plugged into, and that iPod is configured to be updated automatically, a warning dialog box appears, indicating that the iPod is linked to another iTunes Library. You'll be given the option to leave the iPod as is or have its contents replaced by the current computer's iTunes Library. If you choose to leave the iPod as is, you can't add songs to its Library until you open the iPod Preferences window and choose the "manually manage" option (discussed later in this chapter). After you do, you can copy songs freely from that computer's iTunes Library to the iPod.

But that leaves you in a bit of a quandary, for when you return your iPod to the original computer, if you turn on one of the automatic-update options, the songs you copied from the other

continues on next page

computer are erased from the iPod, because they don't exist in the iTunes Library of the original computer. You could simply manage your iPod manually from that day forward, of course, but that pretty well ruptures the convenient relationship between iTunes and the iPod.

Alternatives to this manual-mode scheme? You could copy the song you want from the original CD to both computers (provided that you own the CD, of course). Or you could burn a CD of music files stored on one computer and copy those files to the other computer (again, provided that you own the original material). If you *don't* own the original material—and no, downloading it from an illegal source on the Internet or borrowing your friend's copy of the CD doesn't count—do your conscience a favor and buy the CD or purchase the music from the iTunes Music Store.

Creating and Configuring a Playlist

Before we put any music on your iPod, let's organize it in iTunes. Doing so will make it far easier to find the music you want both in iTunes and on your little portable pal. The best way to organize that music is through the use of playlists.

A *playlist* is simply a group of tracks that you believe should be gathered together in a list. The organizing principle is completely up to you. You can organize songs by artist, by mood, by style, by song length ... heck, if you like, you can create a playlist based on tracks that contain the letter *z* and a prime number. As far as playlists are concerned, you're the boss. Let's look at ways to create those playlists.

Standard playlists

Standard playlists are those that you make by hand. To create one in iTunes, follow these steps:

1. Click the large plus-sign (+) button in the bottom-left corner of the iTunes window, or choose File > New Playlist (Command-N on the Mac, Ctrl-N in Windows).

2. Enter a name for your new playlist in the high-lighted field that appears next to that new play-list in the Source list (**FIGURE 3.5**).

Figure 3.5
Naming a new
playlist

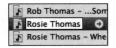

3. Click the Library entry in the Source list, and select the tracks you want to place in the playlist you created.

4. Drag the selected tracks to the new playlist's icon.

5. After you've dragged the tracks you want into your playlist, arrange their order.

   To do so, click the Number column in the main window, and drag tracks up and down in the list. When the iPod is synchronized with iTunes, this is the order in which the songs will appear in the playlist on your iPod.

   If the songs in your playlist come from the same album, and you want the songs in the playlist to appear in the same order in which they do on the original album, click the Album heading.

Playlist from selection

You can also create a new playlist from selected items by following these steps:

1. Select the songs you'd like to appear in the new playlist.

2. Choose File > New Playlist from Selection.

   A new, untitled playlist containing all the selected songs appears in the iTunes Source list.

3. To name the playlist, type the name in the high-lighted field.

Smart Playlists

Smart Playlists are slightly different beasts. These playlists include tracks that meet certain conditions you've defined—for example, Coldplay tracks encoded in AAC format that are shorter than four minutes. Here's how to work the magic of Smart Playlists:

1. In iTunes, choose File > New Smart Playlist.

2. Choose your criteria.

   You'll spy a pop-up menu that allows you to select songs by various criteria—including artist, composer, genre, bit rate, comment, date added, and last played—followed by a Contains field. To choose all songs by Elvis Presley and Elvis Costello, for example, you'd choose Artist from the pop-up menu and then enter **ELVIS** in the Contains field.

   You can limit the selections that appear in the playlist by minutes, hours, megabytes, gigabytes, or number of songs. You may want the playlist to contain no more than 1 GB worth of songs, for example.

You'll also see a Live Updating option. When it's switched on, this option ensures that if you add any songs to iTunes that meet the criteria you've set, those songs will be added to the playlist. If you add a new Elvis Costello album to iTunes, for example, iTunes updates your Elvis Smart Playlist automatically.

3. Click OK.

A new playlist that contains your smart selections appears in iTunes' Source list.

You don't have to settle for a single criterion. By clicking the plus-sign (+) button next to a criterion field, you can add other conditions. You could create a playlist that contains only songs that you've never listened to by punk artists whose names contain the letter *J*.

iTunes includes five Smart Playlists: '90s Music, My Top Rated, Recently Played, Recently Added, and Top 25 Most Played. These playlists have the Live Updating option enabled, which makes it possible for them to update dynamically as conditions change (when you rate more songs, play different tunes, or play other tunes more often, for example).

To see exactly what makes these playlists tick, Mac users can Control-click a Smart Playlist and choose Edit Smart Playlist from the resulting contextual menu. Windows users simply right-click a playlist to see this command.

note In iTunes 4.5, Apple enhanced the Smart Playlist feature in an important way: Now you can tell Smart Playlists to harvest songs only within certain playlists.

Filing with Folders

With iTunes 5 came a new way to file music—in Folders. By invoking the File > New Folder command, you can lump a bunch of playlists together into a single folder. Folders are a great way to keep your playlists separate from your spouse's or to gather groups of similar playlists (All My Jazz Playlists, for example).

Folders don't translate to the iPod, however, as it's incapable of creating nested folders. When you move a folder full of playlists into the iPod, all the songs within all those playlists appear in a single playlist that bears the folder's name.

Tag, You're It

So how does iTunes know about tracks, artists, albums, and genres? Through something called ID3 tags. *ID3 tags* are just little bits of data included in a song file that tell programs like iTunes something about the file—not just the track's name and the album it came from, but also the composer, the album track number, the year it was recorded, and whether it is part of a compilation.

These ID3 tags are the key to creating great Smart Playlists. To view this information, select a track and choose File > Get Info. Click the Info tab in the resulting window, and you'll see fields

continues on next page

for all kinds of things. You may find occasions when it's helpful to change the information in these fields. If you have two versions of the same song—perhaps one is a studio recording and another a live recording—you could change the title of the latter to include *(Live)*.

A really useful field to edit is the Comments field. Here, you can enter anything you like and then use that entry to sort your music. If a particular track would be great to fall asleep to, for example, enter **sleepy** in the Comments field. Do likewise with similar tracks, and when you're ready to hit the hay, create a Smart Playlist that includes "Comment is sleepy." With this technique under your belt, you can create playlists that fit particular moods or situations, such as a playlist that gets you pumped up during a workout.

Moving Music to the iPod (shuffle Excluded)

 The next few pages don't apply to the iPod shuffle, as its iTunes interface is significantly different from the one used for other iPod models. Because it is so different, I've chosen to devote the latter portion of this chapter to the shuffle.

Now that your music is organized, it's time to put it on your 'pod. The conduit for moving music to the iPod is iTunes—which, fortunately, can be fairly flexible in the way it goes about the process.

By default, any tracks in your iTunes Library will be transferred automatically to the iPod when the iPod is plugged into your computer. If there are more tracks in your iTunes Library than will fit on the iPod, iTunes asks to create a subset of your music files and then transfers that subset to your iPod.

There are several ways to configure iTunes so that your iPod is updated when *you* want it to be. It's just as possible to configure iTunes so that just the music you want is copied to your iPod. The key is the iPod Preferences window.

To start, plug your iPod into your computer and launch iTunes. (By default, iTunes launches when you connect the iPod.) The iPod appears in iTunes' Source list (**Figure 3.6**).

Figure 3.6 My iPod in the Source list

▶ 🔲 60GB Color Boy ⬆

To open the iPod Preferences dialog box, select the iPod in the Source list and then click the iPod icon that appears next to the EQ icon in the bottom-right corner of the iTunes window. You can also reach this dialog box by opening the iTunes Preferences window (choose iTunes > Preferences on the Mac or Edit > Preferences in Windows) and clicking the iPod pane.

Within the iPod Preferences window, you'll find, at most, five panes: Music, Podcasts, Photos, Contacts, and Calendars. If you don't have a color iPod, you won't see a Photos pane.

The Music pane

The Music pane contains the options for updating your iPod, as well as for mounting your iPod as a hard disk and displaying album artwork on a color iPod.

Automatically Update All Songs and Playlists

When you choose this option (which is on by default), iTunes updates the iPod to include all the music in the iTunes Library. Any songs currently on the iPod that aren't in the iTunes Library are erased from the iPod.

If you've removed songs from iTunes' Library and want them to remain on your iPod after the update, this option is not for you.

Automatically Update Selected Playlists Only

This option updates only the playlists you've selected. Any songs stored on your iPod that don't belong to the selected playlists are erased when you select this option.

This option is a good one to use when several members of your family share an iPod. It's also a good option for those with large music collections who carry an iPod nano, mini, ROKR phone, or shuffle. This option allows you to chunk up your collection into multiple playlists and then rotate those playlists in and out of your nano, mini, phone, or shuffle by selecting playlists 1, 2, and 3 one month and 4, 5, and 6 the next.

Again, this option isn't a good idea when you don't want items to be removed from your iPod.

Manually Manage Songs and Playlists

Ah, finally—the option to use when you want to add songs to your iPod without removing any tunes from

the device. When you select this option, all the playlists on your iPod appear below the iPod's icon in the
iTunes Source list. To add songs to the iPod, just select
them in the Library or one of iTunes' playlists, and
drag them to one of the iPod's playlists (**FIGURE 3.7**).
Those songs appear at the top of the playlist. To
move a song's position, click the top of the Number
column, and drag the song to where you'd like it to
appear in the list.

Figure 3.7
Moving music
to the iPod
manually

Optionally, you can add songs by genre, artist, or
album by using iTunes' browser. To do so, follow
these steps:

1. In iTunes, choose Edit > Show Browser.

A pane divided into Genre, Artist, and Album columns
appears at the top of iTunes' main window.

2. Click an entry in one of the columns.

If you want to copy all the Kate Bush songs in your
iTunes Library to the iPod, for example, click Ms.
Bush's name in the Artist column. To copy all the
reggae tunes to the iPod, select Reggae in the
Genre column.

3. Drag the selected item to the iPod's icon in the
Source list or to a playlist you've created on the iPod.

To remove songs from the iPod, select the songs you
want to remove within the iPod entry in the Source
list; then press your keyboard's Delete key (or Control-
click on the Mac or right-click for Windows, and
choose Clear from the contextual menu). Mac users
can also drag the songs to the Trash on the Desktop
(or, in the case of OS X, to the Trash in the Dock).

tip When you remove songs from your iPod, you don't remove them from your computer. Unless you select a song in iTunes' Library and delete it, the song is still on your hard drive.

You can even copy entire playlists to other playlists by dragging one playlist icon on top of another. This method works for both iTunes and iPod playlists, though you can't drag a playlist on the iPod to an iTunes playlist and expect the songs to copy over. Songs on the iPod don't copy to your computer (unless you know the trick detailed in Chapter 7.

note When you choose to manage your songs and playlists manually, you'll be told that you have to disconnect the iPod manually—meaning that you have to take action to unmount the thing, rather than simply unplug it from your computer. To do so, you can click the Eject icon next to the iPod's name in the Source list. Alternatively, Mac users can switch to the Finder and drag the iPod to the Trash. When its icon disappears from the Desktop, you can unplug your iPod. Windows users can invoke the Safely Remove Hardware command from the system tray.

The iPod will also tell you when it's ready to be unmounted. When the iPod is mounted on your computer or busy accepting data from an application, the display flashes the international symbol for "Back off, Jack!" (the circle with a line through it), along with a "Do not disconnect" message. When you unmount it properly, the iPod displays a large check mark and the message "OK to disconnect."

Only Update Checked Songs

As its name hints, this option tells iTunes to update those songs that are checked in iTunes' Library. This option can act as a safety measure, ensuring that any songs that are no longer available to iTunes aren't erased from your iPod during an automatic update.

tip **Care to check or uncheck all the songs in a playlist at the same time? On the Mac, hold down the Command key and click any check box in the playlist. In Windows, hold down the Control key and do the same thing. When you uncheck a box, all boxes will be unchecked; check a box, and all boxes will be checked.**

Open iTunes When This iPod Is Attached

With this option enabled, iTunes will launch when you plug the iPod into your computer. Switch it off if you don't want this to happen.

Enable Disk Use

The iPod is, at heart, an elegant storage device that happens to play music. You can mount the iPod as a hard drive on your computer by enabling this option. When the iPod is mounted, you can use it just like a hard drive; copy files to it as you desire.

Display Album Artwork on Your iPod

This option appears if you've plugged an iPod with a color display into your computer. As its name implies, this option determines whether album artwork is displayed on your color iPod.

Podcasts

It would be pretty silly to own a music player called the iPod that didn't play podcasts. Yours does, and this pane determines how podcasts are treated by iTunes and the iPod (**Figure 3.8**).

Figure 3.8 The Podcasts pane of the iPod Preferences window

Automatically Update All Podcasts

When this option is on, iTunes will place new podcasts on your iPod when it synchronizes its music files. The Update pop-up menu at the bottom of the pane determines which podcasts are transferred. You have the choice to update all episodes, checked episodes only, most recent episodes only, and unplayed episodes only. This pop-up menu is a useful way to keep your iPod from getting choked with podcasts you've already listened to or those that are out of date.

Automatically Update Selected Podcasts Only

This works much like the Music pane's Automatically Update Selected Playlists Only option. When this option is switched on, you select just the podcasts that you want transferred to your iPod, and leave the rest in iTunes.

Manually Manage Podcasts

This, too, works like its music counterpart. Enable this option to drag podcasts to your iPod.

Photos (color iPods and iPod nano only)

If you have a color iPod, you can synchronize pictures between your photo library and your iPod. The key to doing so is within the Photos pane of the iPod Preferences window.

Synchronize Photos From option

When you enable this option, you'll see an alert that asks whether you're really sure you want to enable photo support. iTunes does this to warn you that any photos currently on the iPod will be replaced. You don't have the option to manage photos manually; thus, you have to be more careful about accidentally erasing pictures when you plug your color iPod into another computer.

With this option enabled, you can choose a source for your photos. On a Macintosh, you'll see iPhoto listed in the Synchronize Photos From pop-up menu (**Figure 3.9**); you also have the option to choose images from the Pictures folder in your user folder or to select any other folder. This works pretty much as you'd expect.

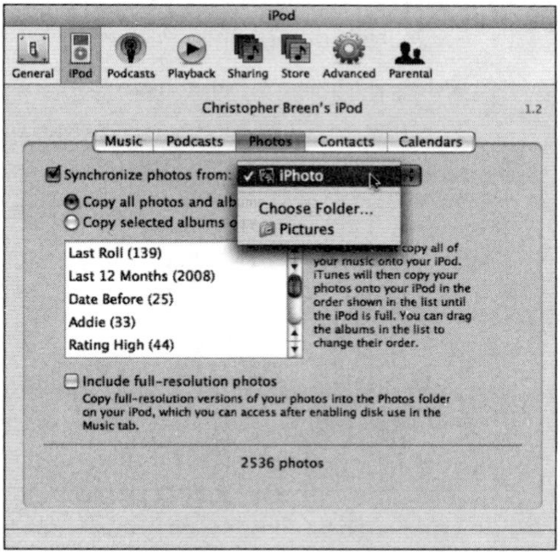

Figure 3.9 You'll see these iPod preferences if you plug in a color iPod.

When you choose iPhoto, the option below the pop-up menu reads Copy All Photos and Albums. When you enable this option, all the pictures in your iPhoto library will be converted and copied to the iPod. You also have the choice to Copy Selected Albums Only. This works much like the Automatically Update Selected Playlists Only option in the Music pane. Regardless of which option you choose, whenever you add new images to a selected album, the iPod automatically updates its photo library when it next synchronizes.

If you choose Pictures from this pop-up menu, the options below it change to Copy All Photos and Copy Selected Folders Only. The principles of iPhoto import apply here as well. If you choose Copy All Photos, iTunes rummages around in this folder and looks for compatible graphics files. If you choose Copy Selected Folders Only, you can direct iTunes to look in only those folders that you select.

Finally, you can select Choose Folder. When you do, up pops a Change Photos Folder Location navigation window. Just traipse to the folder you want to pull pictures from, and click Choose. When you do this, the folder you've chosen replaces Pictures in the pop-up menu.

tip **This is a good way to copy every picture from your hard drive to your iPod. As far as iTunes is concerned, your hard drive is just another folder. Select it as the source folder with the Copy All Photos option selected, and iTunes grabs all the compatible graphics files it can find, converts them, and plunks them onto your iPod.**

This process is no more complicated for Windows users. The main difference is that the Windows version of iTunes offers no iPhoto option (and because there is no version of iPhoto for Windows, that's probably a good thing). Instead, you'll see the option to Copy All or Selected photos from your My Pictures folder or another folder of your choosing.

If you've installed Adobe Photoshop Elements (version 3 or later) or Adobe Photoshop Album on your PC, the Synchronize Photos From pop-up menu also contains entries for these programs, allowing you to import pictures from the albums these programs create (**Figure 3.10**).

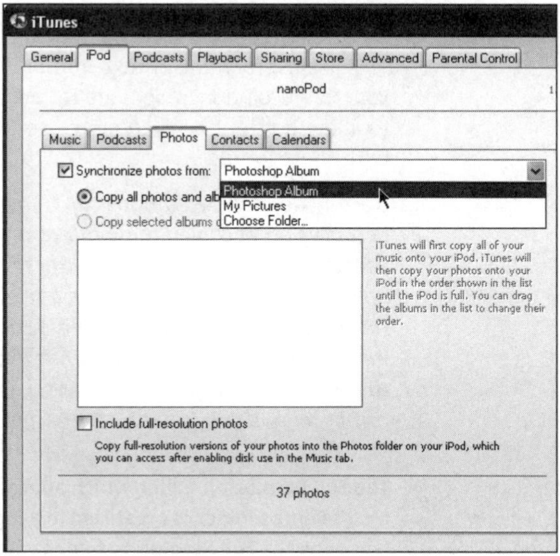

Figure 3.10
Windows users can synchronize photos from their Photoshop Album and Photoshop Elements albums.

tip The tip I proposed for copying all the pictures from your Mac to your iPod works with Windows as well. In this case, choose your C drive as the source. When you do, every compatible graphics file will be converted and copied.

Include Full-Resolution Photos

Near the bottom of the Photos pane of the iPod Preferences window, you'll see the Include Full-Resolution Photos option, followed by this text:

Copy full-resolution versions of your photos into the Photos folder on your iPod, which you can access after enabling disk use in the Music tab.

This is a useful hunk of text, in that it hints at where your full-resolution images are stored, but were room to allow, it might be even more useful if it continued with these words:

Oh, and don't get your hopes up thinking that just because you've copied these full-resolution images to your iPod, you'll be able to view these exact images on your iPod or project them on a television. No, sir (or madam, as the case may be), this option is provided only as a convenient way to transfer your images to the iPod so that you can later attach it to a different computer and copy your pictures from here to there.

note The Full Resolution folder, which appears within the iPod's Photos folder, is organized in a logical way. When you open the Full Resolution folder, you'll see a folder that bears the year the pictures were created. Within this folder are folders marked with the month of creation. Within one of these folders is a folder denoting the day of conception. So the folder hierarchy might look like this: Photos/Full Resolution/2005/2/28/yourphotos.

Contacts

iTunes handles synchronization of contacts and calendars between your computer and iPod. From the Contacts pane on a Macintosh, you can choose to synchronize all your Apple Address Book contacts or just those contacts from selected groups. On a Windows PC, iTunes synchronizes Microsoft Outlook and Outlook Express contacts in the same way—either all contacts or selected groups of contacts.

Calendars

On a Mac, this option lets you synchronize all your iCal calendar events or just those from selected calendars. On a Windows PC, you synchronize your calendars from Outlook.

Moving Music to the iPod shuffle

As I mentioned earlier in the chapter, the iPod shuffle interacts differently with iTunes than does a display-bearing iPod. To begin with, because the shuffle lacks a screen, there's no need to offer options for synchronizing photos, contacts, and calendars. The lack of a screen also means that there's little you can do to navigate a shuffle's music library. You are, in a very real sense, flying blind.

And then there's the shuffle's limited storage space. Because the current shuffles hold just 512 MB or 1 GB, you don't have a lot of extra room for storing large music files. iTunes does its best to keep such files from being placed automatically on your music player.

With these limitations in mind, let's take a look at just what iTunes offers for the shuffle owner.

shuffle preferences

When you attach an iPod shuffle to your Mac or PC, by default, iTunes launches. When it does, the shuffle appears in the iTunes Source list just like any other iPod (save for the fact that its icon looks like a shuffle rather than a full-size iPod). Select that shuffle, and you can open its preferences by clicking the iPod icon at the bottom of the iTunes window or by opening the iTunes Preferences window (choose iTunes > Preferences on the Mac or Edit > Preferences in Windows) and clicking the iPod pane.

What appears is quite different from what you see when you look at a display-bearing iPod's preferences. Instead of seeing a tabbed window, you'll view a single window offering a limited set of options (**Figure 3.11**), which are described in the following sections.

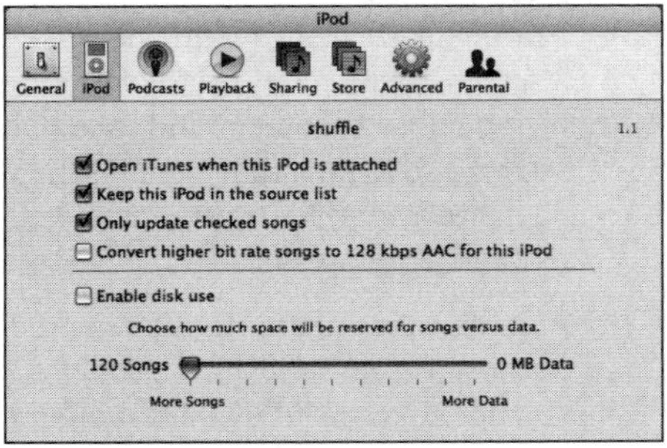

Figure 3.11 The iPod Preferences window shows the shuffle pane when you plug in an iPod shuffle.

Open iTunes When This iPod Is Attached

You can undoubtedly guess what disabling this option does. Uncheck this box if you don't want iTunes to jump to the fore every time you plug in your shuffle.

Keep This iPod in the Source List

This is a new iPod option—and a very convenient one. The idea is that even if you unmount your shuffle, a "virtual" shuffle remains in the Source list. This is essentially a special playlist of the songs currently on the shuffle that you can modify even if the shuffle's not attached to your computer. If you uncheck this option, the shuffle leaves the Source list when you unmount it.

 I particularly like this option because I can bang the Autofill button time and again, and when iTunes comes up with a mix that I like, I can select everything in the playlist, choose File > New Playlist from Selection, and fill my shuffle from this playlist at a later date.

Only Update Checked Songs

If you have a larger iPod, you've seen this option before. This is one way to ensure that certain songs stay on the shuffle and aren't replaced when you next sync it with iTunes.

Convert Higher Bit Rate Songs to 128 Kbps AAC for This iPod

You may recall that in Chapter 1, I mentioned that the shuffle won't accept files encoded in AIFF or Apple Lossless format. iTunes and the shuffle were designed this way so that you wouldn't pack your shuffle with just a few very large song files. Enabling this option allows you to listen to songs encoded in these formats.

iTunes won't automatically place AIFF and Apple Lossless files on your iPod. If you drag such files to the shuffle to place them on the player manually, however, iTunes will automatically convert them to 128 Kbps AAC files when this option is enabled. Your files will remain in their original format on your computer, but a compressed copy will be made specially for the shuffle.

Enable Disk Use

At its heart, the iPod shuffle is little more than a USB key drive—the kind of portable flash-memory drive that you can get at your local Costco for something over $50. If you enable this option, you can mount the shuffle on your computer and use it to store data files as well as music files.

To help ensure that you've got some room left for data files, iTunes includes a slider below this option that allows you to determine how much of the shuffle's storage space will be reserved for songs and how much will go toward data storage. If you set the slider to the halfway point on a 512 MB iPod shuffle, you can fit approximately 60 four-minute 128 Kbps AAC songs and 156 MB of data on your iPod. Double those figures for a 1 GB shuffle.

Autofill pane

Select an iPod shuffle in iTunes' Source list, and you'll notice that the bottom of the iTunes window is suddenly segmented to reveal the Autofill pane (**FIGURE 3.12**). This pane is where you configure iTunes to move music to your shuffle.

Figure 3.12
iTunes reveals the Autofill pane when an iPod shuffle is connected to your computer.

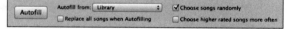

Autofill button

In theory, putting music on your shuffle is very simple. By default, iTunes is set up so that when you click the Autofill button, iTunes grabs a random collection of tracks from your iTunes Library and copies it to your shuffle. But things don't have to work that way. Although the Autofill button, in league with the Autofill From pop-up menu (which you'll hear about in just a sec), is a powerful way to move music to your shuffle, you need never touch it.

Blasphemy? Perhaps. But the only way to ensure that you get *exactly* the music you want on your shuffle is to lay off this button. Instead, if your shuffle has anything on it, select it, select all its contents, and press your computer's Delete key. Then drag just the music you want from your iTunes Library onto the shuffle's icon.

To see the order in which songs will play if the shuffle is set to play from beginning to end, click the Number heading in iTunes' main window. To save that play-list so that you don't lose it when you later fill your shuffle with other music, select everything in the playlist and choose File > New Playlist from Selection. A new playlist will be created in iTunes' Source list that includes all the selected tracks.

If you choose to bang the Autofill button, of course, it does exactly what it says: fills your shuffle with as much as it can of the playlist selected in the Autofill From pop-up menu.

Autofill From pop-up menu

One way to customize your shuffle's contents more carefully is to feed it specific playlists. You might create sets of music that make sense for particular activities—music for your next workout or for a short car trip, for example. When you've created these playlists, you can choose the one you like from the Autofill From pop-up menu (**Figure 3.13**).

Figure 3.13 The Autofill From pop-up menu

Choose Songs Randomly

The shuffle was designed with random play in mind, but you can make it load specific tracks in a specific order by disabling this option. When you do, iTunes will take the playlist selected in the Autofill From pop-up menu and place as much of it as can fit, in order, on the shuffle. When you've flipped your shuffle into "play from beginning to end" mode, the playlist you load will play in that order. This is one way to ensure that the songs in an album you place on the shuffle play in the same order as they do on the album.

Choose Higher Rated Songs More Often

I mean, honestly, what's the use of putting music that you loathe on your shuffle? If you haven't thought of a good reason for rating your music, now you have one. Assign a rating of four or five stars to your favorite tracks, and those tracks are more likely to be moved to your shuffle when this option is enabled.

Replace All Songs When Autofilling

With this option selected, iTunes will wipe out whatever music the shuffle currently holds and replace it with selections from the playlist chosen in the Autofill From pop-up menu. Leaving this option checked is a good way to help ensure that you'll get a fresh crop of music the next time you listen to your shuffle. It's not such a good choice, however, if you want to keep some selections on the shuffle—podcasts, for example—and remove others.

Uncheck this option and check Only Update Checked Songs in the iPod Preferences window, and you've got a whole lot more control. This way, you can uncheck all your podcasts (or other tracks you want to keep) on the shuffle and then click the Autofill button. The stuff you want to keep stays put and is surrounded by new material.

4

The iTunes Music Store

In Chapter 3, you learned how to put the music you own on your iPod. Now it's time to look at a cool way to obtain new music. And by *cool*, I can mean nothing other than Apple's online digital music emporium, the iTunes Music Store. In the following pages, I'll take you on a tour of The Store and show you the best ways to discover and purchase new music.

The One-Stop Shop

Apple has eschewed the typical Internet-commerce model of creating a Web site that users access through a Web browser. Although this model works reasonably well for countless merchants, it invariably requires customers to slog through Web page after Web page to find and pay for the items they desire. Apple wanted a service as immediate as the experience of going to a record store, gathering the music you want, and taking it to the counter.

To replicate this experience, Apple placed The Store inside an application that was already built for music browsing and that many of its customers were likely to be familiar with: iTunes.

Incorporating The Store into iTunes offered several benefits:

- It's easy to access. Just open iTunes (version 4 or later), and click the Music Store icon in the Source list. If your computer is connected to the Internet, the iTunes Music Store interface appears in the main iTunes Window.

tip Starting with iTunes 4.6, Apple made visiting The Store even easier (or, some may say, more annoying). The first time you connect your iPod to your computer or restore your iPod, iTunes launches and displays the iTunes Music Store page. To stop it from doing so, simply click the small X in the information window at the top of the iTunes window, and select a different item in iTunes' Source list.

- It's a cinch to find music. First, enter a search term in the Search Music Store field, located in the top-right corner of the iTunes window. (This term can be an artist, album, or song title, or even a single word.) Then press the Mac's Return key or the PC's Enter key. In very little time, a window appears that includes artists, albums, and song names that match your query. In very little time, a window appears that includes artists, albums, and song names that match your query. If you type **LOUIE** in the Search field, for example, you'll find links to Maggie Louie and Louie Bellson; the Louie James Demons' self-titled album; and, of course, the perennial frat-house favorite, "Louie, Louie."

- It's tough to purchase music you don't want. The Store allows you to hear a 30-second preview of every song it sells. Just highlight the song you want to listen to, and click iTunes' Play button.

- It couldn't be much easier to purchase music. Simply create an Apple account, locate the music you want to buy, and click the Buy Song or Buy Album button next to the pertinent song or album. After iTunes confirms your decision to purchase, it downloads the music to your computer. Songs cost, on average, 99 cents apiece; albums, $9.99.

- Finally, when the music is on your computer, you can copy it to your iPod, play it on up to five computers, and burn it to an audio CD that you can play anywhere you like—all without leaving the iTunes application.

In short, the entire process is about as complicated as ordering and eating a Big Mac and fries (and a whole lot healthier!). Easy to use as it may be, however, The Store has hidden depths. In the following pages, I'll explain all that there is to know about The Store and tell you how you and your iPod can put it to the best use.

Prepare to Shop

Ready to shop? Great. Let's make sure that you have the tools you need to get started. After you have those tools, we'll get you signed up with an account and then take an extensive tour of The Store.

What you need

Of course you need a Mac or Windows PC and a copy of iTunes 4 or later. Although it's not necessary to have an iPod to take advantage of The Store—music purchased at The Store can be played on your computer and burned to CD—the iPod technically is the only portable music player capable of playing music purchased at The Store.

And although you can access The Store via any Internet connection, you'll find it far more fun to shop with a broadband connection. A four-minute song weighs in at around 4 MB. Such a download over a DSL or cable connection takes next to no time at all but can be terribly slow over a poky modem connection.

As these pages go to print, The Store is available in 20 countries. Which store you're allowed to purchase music from depends on the issuing country of your credit card. If you have a credit card issued in Germany, for example, you can purchase music only from the German iTunes Music Store (though you don't physically have to be in Germany to do this—again, the credit card determines where you can shop).

Signing on

You're welcome to browse The Store the first time you fire up iTunes, but to purchase music, you must establish an account and sign in. Fortunately, Apple makes it pretty easy to do so. The process goes like this:

With your computer connected to the Internet, launch iTunes and click the Music Store entry in iTunes' Source list; then click the Sign In button in the top-right corner of the iTunes window. If you have either an Apple ID and password or an AOL screen name and password, enter them and click the Sign In button; otherwise, click the Create Account button.

When creating an account, you'll need to enter a valid email address and create a password. After you've done these things, you'll enter some personal information so that Apple can identify you, if need be.

Finally, after you've traipsed through The Store's terms and conditions, you'll be asked for a credit-card number and your name, address, and phone number. Click Done and . . . well, you're done. You're now a member in good standing.

Tooling Around

As I tap out these words, The Store carries more than 2 million songs. Fortunately, you needn't trudge through an alphabetical list of all these titles. Instead, Apple offers you multiple ways to browse its catalog of compositions. Let's look at The Store's floor plan and the best ways to navigate it.

Navigating The Store's floors

Figure 4.1 The Store's main page

The Store's main page offers a host of links for finding the music you need (**FIGURE 4.1**). Much like a "real" record shop, The Store places the day's most popular picks up front.

Here's what you'll find on the home page.

Primary links

Across the top of the main page, you'll see a banner that changes from time to time. This banner may promote hot new singles or albums, exclusive tracks, or music videos available only at The Store.

Below the banner are side-scrolling windows that contain picture links to New Releases (viewable by genre), Exclusives (tracks not available from other services), Just Added, and Staff Favorites. Click the arrows to the side of each list to scroll forward or backward through the list of selections. In iTunes 5 the New Releases section contains 32 selections; the others have 16 selections each.

tip **On a slowish connection, it takes a while for these lists to scroll. You can scan these categories far more quickly if you click the See All link in the top-right corner of each category.**

Arrayed along the top-left side of the main page are text links that direct you to many of The Store's most interesting features, described in the following sections.

Search links

The two links at the top of the list—Browse Music and Power Search—hint that there are more efficient ways to find music than clicking the song and album titles you see on The Store's home page.

Browse

The Store offers a browser view much like the view
you see when you select your library or a playlist and
choose Edit > Show Browser in iTunes. (In point of
fact, choosing this command produces the same result
as clicking the Browse link.) Click Browse, and iTunes'
browser columns appear, listing Charts, Radio Charts
(we'll get to those in a minute), and The Store's
various Genres in the leftmost column. Click a
Genre entry, and for most genres, a list of subgenres
appears in the second column. (Not all genres offer
subgenres.) Click one of the subgenres, and a list of
artists appears in the third column. Click an artist's
name, and available albums by that artist appear in
the last column. Click an album title, and the music
contained on that album appears in the Results
area below.

The Results area is divided into columns titled Name,
Time, Artist, Album, Genre, and Price (**FIGURE 4.2**). You
can sort the list by any of these criteria by clicking
the appropriate column head. Click Artist, for example,
and the list is sorted alphabetically by artist. Click
Time, and the list is sorted by shortest to longest
playing time.

tip   You'll notice that a right-pointing arrow appears to the
right of entries in both Artist and Album views. Clicking
this arrow allows you to travel to the page devoted to
that album or artist—a great way to explore an album
or an artist's catalog after searching for a single song.

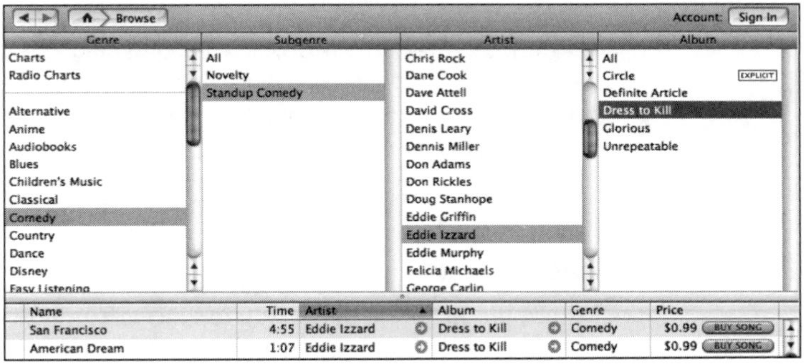

Figure 4.2
The Store's
no-nonsense
browser
view

Power Search

If you want to be a power shopper, you must learn to take advantage of The Store's Power Search function.

When you click the Power Search link on the main page or choose Power Search from the pop-up menu below the magnifying-glass icon in the Search field, you're taken to a page where you can search for music based on such factors as song title, artist, album, genre, and composer. This feature comes in handy when you really want to narrow your search (**FIGURE 4.3**).

Figure 4.3
Power Search

If you performed a simple search for the song "Blue Moon" by entering its title in the Search field, you'd be presented with 902 matches. Even if you search by song title, you'll get just over 345 results. Invoke Power Search, however, and you can narrow things down quite nicely.

If you're interested in vocal renditions of "Blue Moon," for example, enter **BLUE MOON** in the Song field and then choose Vocal from the Genre pop-up menu. Aha—now you get just 22 matches. Had you entered **BILLIE HOLIDAY** in the Artist field, you'd see only five matches.

Feature links

The next group of links directs you to specific features offered by The Store. Some are music-related, whereas others highlight a new or particularly attractive Store add-on.

Podcasts

The Store is a conduit for obtaining podcasts—those do-it-yourself, radiolike broadcasts that you've heard so much about. On the Podcasts page, you'll find a host of podcasts vying for your attention. The structure of the page changes enough that I'm not going to detail what you're likely to find here. Just know that you'll probably see a banner across the top that promotes podcasts deemed interesting by Apple, a Today's Top Podcasts list along the right side that lists that week's most popular 'casts, and a Categories sidebar on the left side that allows you to sort through podcasts by theme—Arts & Entertainment, Business, Comedy, and Public Radio, for example.

When you select a podcast, you'll be taken to a page devoted to it. From this page, you can download single episodes (by clicking the Get Episode button that appears to the right of the podcast) or click the Subscribe button.

When you click Get Episode, iTunes switches to the Podcasts pane, where all your podcasts are listed, and begins downloading the podcast (**Figure 4.4**). You'll see a subject heading for the podcast—KCRW's Le Show, for example—and when you click the triangle next to that heading, you'll view a list of that program's individual shows.

Figure 4.4
The Podcasts pane

Next to a show's subject heading, you'll spy a Subscribe button. When you click this Subscribe button or the Subscribe button in one of The Store's podcast pages, some previous episodes of the now-subscribed show will appear in the Podcasts pane, accompanied by a Get button that, when clicked, allows you to retrieve the shows. When new episodes become available, iTunes automatically downloads them.

If you tire of receiving a particular show, just select its subject heading and click the Unsubscribe button at the bottom of the iTunes window. You'll no longer receive episodes.

Audiobooks

In addition to music, The Store sells audiobooks—"books on tape" items. Click the Audiobooks link, and you'll be taken to a page that looks very much like one of the music pages.

The Audiobooks page is divided into easy-to-understand categories that change every so often. Here, you'll likely find such categories as New & Noteworthy, Great Fiction You May Have Missed, Fiction, Nonfiction, and Classics. These categories (save Great Fiction You May Have Missed) include the kind of material you'd find in a well-stocked airport bookstore—fairly current titles that are likely to appeal to a broad audience. The Classics selections offers titles that many people are required to read by the time they've finished their freshman year of college. The Great Fiction You May Have Missed titles are more obscure.

The left side of the Audiobooks page offers links to more-specific categories of books. Click one of these links, and you'll go to a browser view, where you can search by author.

On the right side of the Audiobooks page, you'll find a list of the day's 20 top-selling books, along with a link to the top 100 books The Store has sold that day. Much like the music top 100 pages, the page of 100 top-selling books includes pictures of the book covers, as well as prices and Buy Book links. To get more information about a particular title, click its picture.

You'll go to a page where you can read a description of the book and listen to a 90-second preview.

Book Burning

Unless the narrator of your purchased audio novel or work of nonfiction reads *very* quickly, the play time for your purchase is likely to be measured in hours. Yet a recordable CD can store only about 80 minutes of audio. How do you cram all that narration onto a single CD?

You can't. When iTunes burns a book to disc, it converts the file to the file format required by audio CDs—a format that consumes 10 MB of hard disk space per minute of stereo audio.

Fortunately, iTunes provides an easy way to record your audio-books to disc. When you select a file that will exceed the recording capacity of an audio CD and ask iTunes to burn a disc, the program offers to split the file into lengths that can fit on a CD. (If you must know, each segment is 1 hour, 19 minutes, and 56 seconds.) When iTunes fills one CD, it spits it out and asks for another blank disc. It continues to spit and ask until it finishes burning the entire file to disc.

The resulting discs won't be named in an intuitive way—"War and Peace" I, II, and III, for example. Rather, each will simply read "Audio CD" when you insert it into your Mac or PC. For this reason, you should keep a Sharpie at the ready to label each disc as it emerges from your CD burner.

iMix

iMix is your chance to inflict your musical values on the rest of the world by publishing a playlist of your favorite (or, heck, your least-favorite) songs. When you click the iMix link, you're taken to a page that contains three columns marked Top Rated, Most Recent, and Featured. Click an album cover to view (and purchase, if you like) the songs in it.

As enjoyable as it may be to view others' iMixes, it's more fun to create your own. You can do so by following these steps:

1. Create a new playlist in iTunes, and give it a really cool name.

   The cooler the name, the more likely others are to view your iMix.

2. Cruise through your iTunes Library, and drag into it songs you'd like to publish in an iMix.

   Note that your iMix can contain only songs available for purchase from The Store. If the iMix contains songs that are not available at The Store, those songs won't appear in the published playlist.

3. Round out your list with songs at The Store that you don't own.

   An iMix doesn't require that you actually own the music you're recommending; you can drag previews of any of The Store's songs or audiobooks into a playlist in iTunes' Source list. Feel free to add these previews to your iMix playlist.

4. Click the arrow to the right of your playlist's name.

   Clicking this arrow produces a dialog box that warns you that you're about to create and upload an iMix.

5. Click Create.

   You'll be taken to The Store, and iTunes' main window will show you a picture of the cover of your album (a collage of album covers for the songs you've included).

6. Edit the title and description to suit your iMix.

7. Click Publish.

Your iMix will be published to The Store and will remain there for one year. You'll receive an email confirmation of the iMix's publication.

8. Tell a friend.

The window that tells you that your iMix has been published also offers the Tell a Friend button. Click this button to view the Tell a Friend screen, where you can send an email announcement to whoever you like. When your announcement has been sent, you have the option to send another.

9. Click Done when you're finished.

Your iMix won't appear in the Most Recent column right away. Apple vets these things, and if it doesn't approve of your iMix's title, it won't appear.

To search The Store's iMixes, click the iMix link, and, in the resulting iMix page, enter your search term in the page's Search For field. You'll be transported to a page that includes any iMixes that match your search.

Billboard Charts

Clicking the Billboard Charts link takes you to The Store's browser view. Apple, in league with *Billboard* magazine, has collected the Billboard Hot 100, Billboard Top Country, and Billboard Top R&B lists for the past umpteen years (*umpteen* in this case meaning as far back as 1946).

These charts list only those songs that are available at The Store, so you'll find gaps in them. During the mid- and late '60s, for example, the Beatles owned many of the top spots on the Billboard charts, yet the lads from Liverpool appear nowhere in these charts. When a song isn't available, numbers are simply skipped. The top three spots in 1968's Hot 100 are missing, for example.

Radio Charts

If you've been following along at The Store while reading this chapter, you know that the same browser view that displays Billboard Charts is also the home of Radio Charts. It works this way:

When you click Radio Charts, you'll see a list of cities in the browser's second column. Click a city, and a list of FM radio stations in that city appears in the browser's third column. Click a radio station, and a list of 60 or fewer songs available at The Store that are routinely played on that station appear below. These lists not only help you learn what music is topping the charts from coast to coast, but they're also a nice way to find a song you've heard on the radio and failed to get the name of. Chances are that if a song's in constant rotation, it will appear in iTunes' Radio Charts.

Video links

The next logical step for The Store is to move into the movie market, selling videos as well as music. That day has yet to dawn, but Apple's toe is definitely in the water, as indicated by The Store's Music Videos and Movie Trailers links.

Music Videos

The Music Videos link takes you to a page of ... well, music videos. Click a video, and you're offered the option to watch the small or large version of a QuickTime video that's streamed to your computer. (If you have a small monitor, you may have to scroll the window to see the size buttons.)

Viewing a video requires that you have Apple's QuickTime installed (as of course you do, because iTunes requires it). Choose the version you want, and a black movie window appears, after which the movie begins to stream across your Internet connection. When enough of the movie has been downloaded to ensure smooth playback of the entire thing, the movie begins playing in iTunes' main window rather than in the Artwork window, where album art and movies stored in the iTunes browser are normally displayed.

You'll find two links on these video pages: one in the video window that will take you to the artist's page and the traditional purchase/preview link to the song played in the video.

Movie Trailers

Apple offers movie trailers at The Store in part to sell soundtrack albums. When you click the Movie Trailers link, you'll be taken to a page that displays links to current movie trailers; trailers for recently released DVDs; and, of course, links to popular soundtrack albums available for purchase at The Store.

Gift and support links

The final group of links in the first pane of The Store's home page direct you to an area for bestowing the gift of music on your nearest and dearest, an area for redeeming those gifts, and a Support link that directs you to The Store's Web page.

Allowance

An iTunes allowance can best be described as a gift certificate (which I'll describe in a moment) that keeps on giving. After you create an allowance, the recipient of your largesse will have his or her Store credit bumped up by the amount that you've designated (values include $10 to $100 in $10 increments, $150, and $200) on the first day of each month. Just as when you purchase a gift certificate, your credit card will be charged, not the recipient's.

Creating an iTunes allowance works this way:

1. Click the Allowance link.

2. In the Set up an iTunes Allowance window before you, you'll be asked to provide your name, the recipient's name, and a value for the monthly allowance. You'll also be given the option to send the allowance now or wait until the first of the next month. If your recipient doesn't have an Apple ID, you must create one for him or her. Otherwise, enter the ID in the Apple ID field. You can also append a personal message.

3. Click Continue.

You'll be asked to enter your Apple ID and password. Then you move on to the Confirm Your Purchase screen.

4. After you've checked everything twice, click Buy.

The next screen tells you that the allowance has been created.

5. Click Done to return to the Apple Account Information page.

After you've created an allowance, a new Manage Allowances button appears on your Apple Account Information page. When you click this button, you go to the Edit Allowances page, where you can add allowances or suspend or revoke any that you've created. When you revoke an allowance, any balance placed in the account remains; it won't be credited back to you.

If you think you're going to reinstate that allowance—when your daughter starts making her bed again, for example—use the Suspend button. If you click Remove, you won't be able to put that allowance back into service; you must create a new one. To reactive a suspended account, return to this screen, and click the Activate button next to the account name. When you do, a dialog box will appear, asking whether you'd like to send the allowance immediately or wait until the first of the next month.

Gift Certificates

Click the Gift Certificates link to purchase electronic certificates in denominations ranging from $10 to $200 that you email to the objects of your affection.

(You can also redeem gift certificates within this window.)

To let your loved ones know how much you care (or how little you care to jump in the car and go to a bricks-and-mortar music store), follow these steps:

1. Click the Gift Certificates link.

2. In the iTunes Gift Certificates window before you, click the Buy Now button.

3. In the next window, provide your name, the recipient's name, and the recipient's email address; choose a value for the certificate; and, if you want to, enter a personal message.

Optionally, you can choose to print a gift certificate or send the gift certificate by snail mail (at least, you can with the U.S. iTunes Music Store). Clicking the Send via U.S. Mail button launches your Web browser and takes you to an Apple Store page, where you can create a gift certificate that Apple will mail to your recipient.

4. Click Continue.

You'll be asked to confirm that the information you entered was correct.

5. After you've checked everything twice, click Buy.

The next screen tells you that the certificate has been sent.

6. Click Buy Another, if you're feeling particularly generous, or click Done to return to the Apple Account Information page.

iTunes Music cards

Apple and retailers such as Target also sell prepaid
iTunes Music cards. If you can't obtain a Store
account because you lack a credit card or are looking
for an easy-to-give gift, one of these cards is a nice
way to go. If you've received such a prepaid card and
want to redeem it, just click the iTunes Music Cards
link, enter the 16-digit code that appears on the back
of the card, and click Redeem. In next to no time, your
account will be credited.

Redeem

To redeem any gift certificates sent to you, click this
link. When you do, iTunes' main window will be taken
up with the Enter Code screen, where you enter a
12-digit gift certificate code to redeem your Store credit.

**Gift certificates can be redeemed only from the store
from which they were issued. A gift certificate purchased
at the German iTunes Music Store cannot be redeemed
at the U.S. iTunes Music Store, for example.**

Support

With this book at your side (or, better yet, open in
front of your face), you shouldn't need to click The
Store's Support link, but should you come across a
problem that's arisen since the publication of this
edition, click this link to be taken to Apple's iTunes
Support Web page. Here, you'll find answers to
frequently asked questions about both iTunes and
The Store.

iTunes Originals

iTunes Originals are albums created specifically for The Store by such artists as Moby, Sarah McLachlan, Aimee Mann, and the Wallflowers. These albums feature album cuts, live performances, and interview clips in which the artist offers insights into the album's music tracks.

iTunes Essentials

Although you can purchase entire albums from The Store (and are occasionally required to purchase an entire album to get all the songs on it), it's mostly a song-based enterprise. By this, I mean that The Store encourages you to pick and choose just the pieces of music you like.

Given this idea, it makes sense that Apple would offer compilations of songs, organized by some catchy sort of theme—Women in Bluegrass, Animation Classics, and It Came from TV!, for example. Apple calls these compilations iTunes Essentials, and you'll find a listing of recent iTunes Essentials smack-dab on The Store's home page.

Yes, these are essentially Apple's own iMixes—collections of songs the folks who work at The Store think you'll like (**FIGURE 4.5**). Unlike most of The Store's other albums, these compilations don't give you a discount. If an iTunes Essential contains 25 songs, you pay $24.75, or 99 cents per song.

Figure 4.5 iTunes Essentials offer three levels of themed music.

iTunes Essentials are offered in four configurations: The Basics, Next Steps, Deep Cuts, and Complete Set. As their names indicate, The Basics includes the most obvious songs that fit a particular theme, Next Steps offers slightly more obscure tracks, Deep Cuts hits the fringes, and Complete Set offers all songs in the previous three categories.

Celebrity Playlists

If you'd like to know what rocks the worlds of Dane Cook, Cowboy Troy, Patti Smith, and The Presidents of the United States (no, I'm not exactly sure whether it was Millard Fillmore or Gerald Ford who picked the tunes for this particular list), click these links. The

resulting page offers a list of tunes an artist thinks
worthy. Of course, you can preview and purchase
songs—either individually or the entire list—directly
from this page.

Top of the pops

The right side of the main page offers its share of
navigation links as well. Here, you'll find links to Today's
Top Songs and Today's Top Albums. These lists include
the top 10 recently downloaded songs and albums.
Should you care to view the top 100 downloaded
songs or top 100 downloaded albums, click the Top
100 Songs and Top 100 Albums links, respectively.

note These Top lists don't point to the best music around.
Remember, the technical requirements of The Store
necessarily determine who shops there. The Store's
clientele is confined to Macintosh owners running Mac
OS X and Windows users running Windows XP or 2000,
most of whom have a reasonably fast connection to the
Internet. This demographic doesn't favor fans of Perry
Como or Bix Beiderbecke, so don't be disappointed if
your favorite artists never rise to the top of the charts.

A practical pop-up

Given the links to New Releases, Exclusives, Pre-Releases,
Staff Favorites, videos, iTunes Essentials, Billboard and
radio charts, Celebrity Playlists, and Today's Top Songs
and Albums, as well as access to the Search and
Browse functions, you should be well on your way,

right? Perhaps. But don't leave the main page without checking out the Choose Genre pop-up menu.

You'll find this menu in the top-left corner of the main page. It's a great tool to use when you're in the mood for a particular style of music. Just click the menu and pick the genre that appeals to you, such as Folk or Dance.

Choosing an item from the Genre menu takes you to a page devoted to that genre. This page is laid out similarly to the main page, containing at least New Releases, Staff Favorites, and Just Added sections, plus an Up & Coming section where appropriate. Some genre pages include subcategory listings. On the Folk page, for example, you'll find links to '60s folk music.

The Today's Top Songs and Today's Top Albums lists change to reflect the most popular songs and albums within that genre. On these pages, you'll also find links to the top 100 songs and top 100 albums for that genre.

The Search Music Store field

Looking for a song, artist, or album in a hurry? Click in the Search field in the top-right corner of the iTunes window, enter your query, and press Return or Enter. After a few moments, matching items divided by artists, albums, and songs will appear. Within this window, you can narrow your search by clicking Music, Audiobooks, or Podcasts in the top-left section of the window and then Artist, Album, or Name in the top-middle section.

The way home

Should you ever wander into one of the scarier sections of The Store (say, the polka aisle), it's easy to find your way back to the main page. Simply click the Home icon at the top of the iTunes window, and you're transported to the main page (**Figure 4.6**).

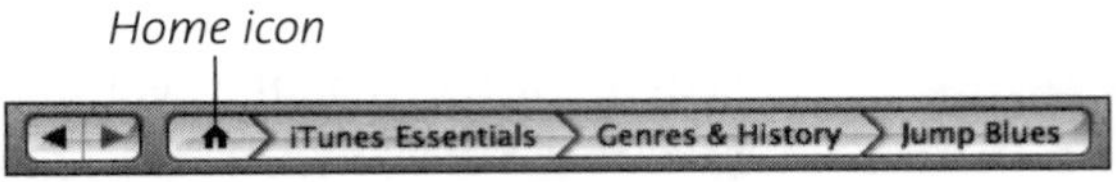

Home icon

Figure 4.6
iTunes'
navigation
controls make
it easy to find
your way home.

Next to the Home icon, you'll see a path from your present location to the main page—Home/Rock/ Peter Gabriel/Secret World Live, for example. To move up a level or two, simply click one of the entries in this hierarchy.

Another way to retrace your steps is to use the Back and Forward buttons, just to the left of the Home icon. These buttons are similar to the Back and Forward buttons in your Web browser. Click the Back button to move to the page you viewed previously. If you've backtracked and want to go forward again, click the Forward button.

Audio appetizers: Previewing songs

How many times have you purchased a CD because you liked one track and discovered that the rest of the disc was utter dreck? Thanks to The Store's Preview feature, those days are over.

You can listen to 30 seconds of every song available from The Store. I can't stress strongly enough how cool this is. It's like waltzing into the kitchen of any restaurant on earth, whipping out a spoon, and taking a nibble of every dish on the menu.

Previewing music is easy. Just select a song title and initiate the preview by clicking iTunes' Play button, double-clicking the song title, or pressing the spacebar on your keyboard. Your computer will access the Web, download the preview, and play 30 seconds of the song you selected.

To preview the previous or next song in a list while a preview is playing, press the left-arrow key to play the previous song or the right-arrow key to play the next song.

Learning about new music

Suppose you're slavishly devoted to a particular artist. Wouldn't it be great if someone from The Store called you up to tell you that Your Very Favorite Artist has a brand-new track ready for download? Recent versions of iTunes offer the next-best thing.

Just click an artist's name to be taken to that artist's page. Glance at the top-right corner of the page, and you'll see the Artist Alert link. Click this link, and up pops The Store's sign-in dialog box. Enter your Apple ID and password, click Add, and click OK in the confirmation dialog box; the artist is added to your list of faves. When a new song from this artist becomes available, you'll receive an email alerting you to that fact.

Getting the Goods

Now that you have an account and can find your way around The Store, it's time to stop manhandling the merchandise and actually buy something. You'll be amazed by how easy (and addictive) this can be.

The pick-and-pay method

The pick-and-pay method is akin to going to a record store, picking up a CD, taking it to the counter, purchasing the disc, returning to the store to pick another CD, purchasing it, going back to the store once again, and ... well, you get the idea. You pay as you go. This is how The Store operates by default. Pick-and-pay works this way:

1. Pick your Poison (or Prince, P-Funk, or Procol Harum).

Using any of the methods I suggested earlier, locate a song or album that you desperately need to own.

2. Click the Buy Song or Buy Album button.

To purchase a song, click the Buy Song entry in the Price column that appears in iTunes' main window. To purchase an album, look in the first pane of the browser and then click the Buy Album button. The price of your purchase is listed next to each of these buttons.

 At times, you can't download an entire album. Instead, The Store may list a partial album—one from which you can purchase only individual songs.

3. Enter your Apple ID or AOL screen name and password in the resulting window.

4. Click the Buy button.

Just to make sure you weren't kidding around when you clicked the Buy button, a new window asks you to confirm your intention to make your purchase. Should you care to banish this window forevermore, check the Don't Warn Me About Buying (Songs/Albums) Again check box.

If you've decided not to purchase the song or album, click Cancel and go on with your life.

5. Click the Buy button again.

The song or album you purchased begins down-loading, and you're charged for your purchases. As each song downloads, it appears in the Purchased Music playlist, accessible from iTunes' Source list. The progress of the download is displayed at the top of the iTunes window.

The shopping-cart method

If you intend to bulk up your music library signifi-cantly in a single shopping session, you might find the pick-and-pay method tedious. The Store offers an alternative—piling all your music into a single shop-ping cart and checking out in one fell swoop. To do so, follow these steps:

1. Choose iTunes > Preferences on your Mac or Edit > Preferences on your PC.

2. Click the Store icon in the resulting window.

3. Select the Buy Using a Shopping Cart option.

4. Click OK to dismiss the window.

A Shopping Cart entry appears in iTunes' Source list.

5. Whirl around The Store until you find a song or album you want to purchase.

The buttons in the Price column and below the album entry read Add Song and Add Album, respectively.

6. Click the Add Song or Add Album button to add a song or album to your shopping cart.

7. Repeat steps 5 and 6 until you can shop no more.

8. Click the Shopping Cart entry in the Source list.

The main iTunes window displays all the songs and albums you've piled into your cart. (Album titles appear with a triangle next to them. Click the triangle to reveal the contents of the album.)

At the bottom of the window, you'll see the total you'll owe if you proceed. This total does not include sales tax (which—yes—you will be charged).

9. Remove any songs and albums you don't want.

10. Buy your music.

Within the shopping cart, you can buy songs or albums individually by clicking Buy Song or Buy Album, or buy everything in the cart by clicking the Buy Now button at the bottom of the iTunes window.

The items in your shopping cart remain there even when you log out of The Store or quit iTunes. To remove them permanently, either buy them or click the Remove button next to each item.

Limited for Your Protection

With every intention of creating a successful distribution system, Apple has tried to address the desires of both consumers and the music industry. Consumers should be pleased that they're allowed to play music purchased at The Store on a variety of devices: computer; portable music player (the iPod); and any commercial CD player, including the ones in your home stereo, boom box, and car. And the music industry's fears of rampant piracy should be calmed because consumers can play that music on a limited number of computers; purchased music files are linked to the person who purchased them; only so many copies of a particular playlist can be burned to CD; and by default, the only music player that can play that music is the iPod.

Following are the specific restrictions Apple imposes on purchased music:

• Purchased music is encoded in a protected version of Dolby Laboratories' Advanced Audio Coding (AAC) format, which bears the .m4p extension (versus the .m4a extension of the standard AAC files that iTunes 4 can create). These files are encoded in a way that makes pirating difficult.

• You may play purchased music on up to five computers, which can be a mix of Macs and Windows PCs. All these computers must be authorized by Apple. If you attempt to play purchased music on an unauthorized computer, you'll be instructed to register the computer online before you can play the music. I describe the ins and outs of authorization in "Play it" later in this chapter.

continues on next page

- You may burn up to seven CD copies of a particular playlist that contains purchased music. When you change that playlist—add or subtract a song, for example—you may burn another seven copies. Change the playlist again for another seven burns.

- You cannot burn purchased music on CDs formatted as MP3 discs.

- The name and Apple ID of the person who purchased the music are embedded in each purchased song. Apple does this to discourage buyers from making those songs widely available on the Web (and to trace songs to the rightful owner, should they find their way to the Web).

- You can download purchased music only one time. If you need to download it again—because your hard drive crashed, for example, and you lost your music library—you must purchase it again. This is reason enough to back up your music library (preferably by burning it to CD).

- All purchases are final. If you download Highway 9's "Heroine," thinking that it's the Velvet Underground's "Heroin," you're stuck with it.

- You can play purchased music on as many iPods as you like, as long as those iPods are running iPod Software 1.3 Updater or later. Earlier versions of the iPod software won't recognize AAC-encoded music (either standard AAC encoding or the protected AAC format used for purchased music).

Playing with Your Purchase

After the purchased music has found a home on your hard drive, you have several ways to put it to work.

Play it

If you're like 99 percent of the people who shop at The Store, the first thing you'll want to do is play the music you've purchased. When you first play a purchased song, iTunes checks to see that your computer is authorized to play purchased music.

As you may recall, you are allowed to play purchased music on up to five computers. When you play a purchased song for the first time, iTunes checks to see whether the computer is authorized to play purchased music. If so, the music plays back with no problem. If the computer hasn't been authorized, you'll be prompted for your Apple ID or AOL screen name and password. That name and password, along with some information that identifies your computer, are sent to Apple, where that Mac or PC is counted against your limit of five authorizations.

If you've used up your authorizations on five other computers, you'll be notified that you must deauthorize one of your computers before you're allowed to play the purchased music. Fortunately, deauthorizing a computer is as simple as choosing Advanced > Deauthorize Computer in iTunes. When you choose this command, your computer connects to the Internet, and Apple's database is updated to reflect the deauthorization of that particular computer.

After you deauthorize a computer, of course, you can't use it to play back purchased music until you authorize it again. (Yes, this means that if you own more than five computers and intend to play purchased music on all of them, you're going to spend some time playing the deauthorization shuffle.)

 Reformatting the computer's hard drive (or replacing that hard drive) does not deauthorize the machine. Before passing your computer along to someone else, be sure to deauthorize it.

Burn it

People play music on all kinds of devices and in all kinds of environments—on computers, boom boxes, home stereos, and portable music players, and in cars, boats, and planes. (I've even seen a system that allows you to play music in your hot tub.) Forcing you to listen to music only on your computer is silly. And because Apple Computer is anything but silly, it made sure that you'd be able to take your purchased music with you on something other than an iPod, iBook, or Windows PC. It does so by allowing you to burn purchased music to CD.

When you do so, the .m4p files are converted to red-book audio files—the file format used by commercial audio CDs. These CDs are not copy-protected in any way and behave just like regular ol' audio CDs. Pop 'em into a standard CD player and press Play, and out comes the music.

As I indicated earlier in this chapter, burning your music to CD involves a few limitations. You can burn up to seven copies of a particular playlist. If you attempt to burn an eighth copy, you'll be told that you can't. If you alter that playlist after the seventh burn—by adding or removing a song—you can burn another seven copies. Alter that playlist, and you get seven more copies.

5

The Informational iPod

By now, you probably realize that the iPod is the world's greatest portable music player. But take a quick scroll through the Extras screen of any display-bearing iPod, and you'll get the idea that the iPod is more than a music player. Here, you'll find the Contacts, Calendar, and Notes entries, which hint that your iPod is ready to offer up a phone number, remind you of an upcoming appointment, or recall your Aunt Vilma's recipe for Swedish meatballs. Though no substitute for a Palm device (or even for some of today's more sophisticated mobile phones), the iPod can perform a reasonably convincing impression of a personal information manager. In these pages, I'll show you how to take best advantage of these features by composing, moving, and synchronizing your contacts, calendars, and notes with your iPod.

Making iContact

The first informational feature to appear on early iPods was Contacts. Here's how they work.

Viva vCard

I don't mean to geek you out with technical jargon, but to understand how the iPod works its contact magic, it's helpful to know that, like your computer, the iPod supports something called the *vCard standard*. This is a scheme concocted a couple of decades ago that allows you to read contact files created on a variety of devices—a computer, mobile phone, or Palm device, for example. The idea is that I can create a contact with my Mac's copy of Address Book and email it to my sister who uses a Windows PC, and she can view that contact in her copy of Microsoft Outlook.

Apple designed the iPod so it also supports vCards. Just plunk that vCard into the right folder on your iPod, and when you next click your iPod's Contacts entry, the rich details of that person, place, or thing will be revealed.

Note that the iPod won't display every bit of data that the vCard standard supports. The iPod can't currently display a contact's picture, for example. It can, however, display the following items:

- **CONTACT'S FORMATTED NAME.** Bubba Jones, for example.
- **CONTACT'S NAME.** The name as it appears in the contact (Jones, Bubba, Dr., for example).

- **CONTACT'S ADDRESS(ES).** The address types supported by vCard (business, home, mailing, and parcel).

- **CONTACT'S TELEPHONE NUMBER(S).** The phone numbers supported by vCard.

- **CONTACT'S EMAIL.** The email addresses in the contact.

- **CONTACT'S TITLE.** Dr., Ms., Mr., and so on.

- **CONTACT'S ORGANIZATION.** The company name displayed in the contact.

- **CONTACT'S URL.** The Internet address contained in the contact.

- **CONTACT'S NOTE.** The note field in the contact.

vCard support wouldn't mean much if common applications didn't support it. Fortunately, the universal nature of the standard means that most information-management and email applications you're likely to run across support vCard. As this book goes to press, vCard support is present on the Mac in OS X's Address Book, Qualcomm's Eudora, Bare Bones Software's Mailsmith, Microsoft's Entourage email clients, and Palm's Palm Desktop 4.x and Now Software's Now Contact information managers. For Windows, you'll find vCard supported in such mainstays as Windows' Address Book, Microsoft Outlook, and Palm Desktop.

Working with contacts

Now that you understand the underlying structure of the iPod's contacts, you're ready to put them to practical use. In the following pages, you'll create contacts in various applications and export them to the iPod.

The manual method: Macintosh

Much like their paper counterparts, vCards are amenable to being dropped where they can be most helpful. In the case of vCards, this means that you can drag them from their host application (Mac OS X's Address Book application or Microsoft Entourage) onto your Mac's Desktop or into another vCard-friendly application.

Wouldn't it be swell if you could drop them into your iPod just as easily?

You can. Here's how, using Apple's Address Book:

1. Open Address Book.

You'll find it in Mac OS X's Applications folder at the root level of your startup drive. All the contacts appear in the main window.

2. To select all the contacts, press Command-A; to select individual contacts, Command-click each contact you want to select.

Alternatively, you can select your contacts and choose File > Export vCards. The selected contacts will be placed in a single vCard.

3. If your iPod's not connected to your Mac, make the connection, and wait for its icon to appear on the Desktop.

4. Configure your iPod so that it mounts on the Mac's Desktop as an external hard drive (by enabling the Enable Disk Use option in the iPod Preferences window's General pane).

5. Double-click the iPod icon on the Desktop to open the iPod's hard drive, where you'll see a Contacts folder.

6. Drag your vCard files into the iPod's Contacts folder (**Figure 5.1**).

Figure 5.1
Copying a vCard file to the iPod's Contacts folder

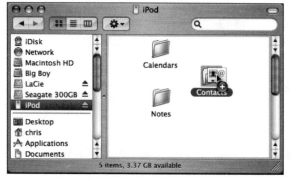

7. Disconnect your iPod, and navigate to the Contacts screen to view your contacts.

The manual method: Windows

Moving contacts manually from Windows applications to the iPod isn't terribly different from performing the operation on the Mac. Here's how to go about it with Windows' Address Book:

1. Launch Address Book.

2. If it's not already selected, choose Main Identity's Contacts in the Address Book window's left pane.

3. Press Ctrl-A to select all the contacts, hold down the Ctrl key while clicking noncontiguous contacts to select multiple contacts individually, or hold down the Shift key while clicking two contacts (those two contacts and all contacts between them will be selected).

4. Drag the contacts to the desktop.

5. Mount your iPod and open it by double-clicking its icon in the My Computer window.

6. Drag and drop your contacts into the iPod's Contacts folder.

Your contacts have been moved to the iPod as individual vCard files.

7. Unmount your iPod by clicking the iPod icon in the system tray and choosing Unmount from the resulting contextual menu.

8. Wait for the iPod to reboot; then navigate to the Contacts screen.

The contacts you copied are displayed in the Contacts list.

The process I've just outlined is fairly common across applications. Whether you're using Palm Desktop, Microsoft's Entourage or Outlook, or some other email client or contact manager, you'll likely find a way to drag contacts from the program to the desktop as vCards, or you'll locate an Export command some-where in the program's File menu that allows you to export your contacts as vCards.

The nice thing is that it may not be necessary to do any of this dragging and exporting. iTunes 5 offers

a way for Mac and Windows users to sync their
Address Book contacts with their iPods.

Sorting Your Contacts

The iPod is just the tiniest bit flexible in how it lets you view your
contacts—letting you sort one way and view the other. To set
your contact sorting and display preferences, highlight the Settings
entry in the iPod's main screen, press Select, and scroll down to
Contacts. Press Select again, and you'll find the Sort and Display
options. Each option allows you to select First and Last or Last and
First, thus allowing you to sort by last name but display your
contacts' first name first and last name . . . well, last.

The automated method: Macintosh

Once upon a time, a program called iSync was respon-
sible for syncing contacts and calendars with an iPod.
No longer. iTunes now offers this feature. Here's how
it works:

1. Plug your iPod into your Mac.

2. Choose iTunes > Preferences, click the iPod entry,
and then click the Contacts tab.

3. Enable the Synchronize Address Book Contacts
option.

To place all the contacts in Address Book on your
iPod, make sure that the Synchronize All Contacts
option is enabled. If you'd rather place only certain
contacts on the iPod, enable the Synchronize
Selected Groups Only option, and in the list

below, choose the groups whose contacts you'd like to copy to the iPod (**Figure 5.2**). You may want only your business contacts or friends and family contacts on your iPod, for example. Grouping those contacts in Address Book and then selecting those groups in iTunes is the way to do it.

Figure 5.2 The Contacts pane in the Macintosh version of iTunes

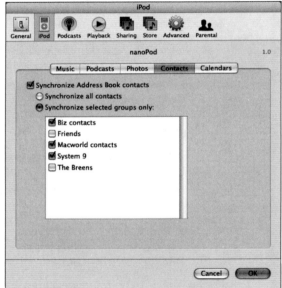

4. Choose File > Update *nameofipod* (where *nameofipod* is your iPod's name).

iTunes will synchronize the selected contacts between your Mac and the iPod.

note If you've configured your iPod to be updated manually, choosing the Update command updates only your contacts, calendars, and—if iTunes is set to update them automatically—podcasts. iTunes won't overwrite the iPod's music library with its contents.

I Need Contact!

If, like many Mac users, you've carefully squirreled away your contacts in Microsoft's Entourage or Palm's Palm Desktop, you may be disappointed that iTunes works only with Address Book. But as Aristotle was so fond of saying, "It's no use crying over spilled goat's milk."

If you want to use iTunes and don't care to pay for a third-party utility, you must use Address Book. Fortunately, it's not difficult to move contacts from either program into Address Book. Here's how:

Entourage

1. In Mac OS X 10.2 or earlier, open the AppleScript folder inside Mac OS X's Applications folder, and double-click the Script Menu.menu item. In Mac OS X 10.3 and later, double-click the Install Script Menu application in this same location.

This places an AppleScript menu in the Mac's menu bar.

2. Choose AppleScript > Mail Scripts; then choose the Import Addresses script from the submenu.

When you run this script, a window appears that gives you the option to import addresses from Entourage, Outlook Express, Palm Desktop, Eudora, Claris Emailer, or Netscape into Mac OS X's Address Book.

3. Choose Entourage, and click OK.

The script will run and copy your Entourage addresses to Mac OS X's Address Book.

continues on next page

Palm Desktop (version 4 and later)

You can also move Palm Desktop contacts to Address Book with the script I just described, but if you'd like to try a different method, follow these steps:

1. Launch Palm Desktop, and choose Window > Address List.

2. In the resulting Address List window, select the contacts you'd like to move to OS X's Address Book.

3. Choose File > Export.

4. In the resulting Export: Palm Desktop window, name your file, select the Desktop as the destination for your saved file, and choose vCard from the Format pop-up menu.

5. Click the Export button.

   A vCard containing all the selected contacts is saved to the Desktop.

6. Open Address Book, and drag the vCard into either the Group or Name portion of the window.

   In a flash, your contacts appear in Address Book, ready for exporting to your iPod via iTunes.

Older contact managers

Those who use older contact managers, such as TouchBase and DynoDex, may believe that they've been left out of the party. Not so. Although these contact managers won't run in Mac OS X (or, likely, in Mac OS 9), you can still pull their data into Address Book. The means for doing so is Palm Desktop.

Palm Desktop began life as Claris Organizer, and it retains the file compatibility that it had in its Claris incarnation. Just use Palm Desktop's Import command to open your old contact-manager file (you may need to move a few fields around during the import process to make the data line up correctly) and then export it as a vCard file.

The automated method: Windows

With iTunes 5, Apple finally brought contact and calendar synchronization to the Windows version of the program. iTunes for Windows will synchronize Outlook's and Outlook Express' contacts and calendars with your iPod. To make it do so, you follow a procedure similar to the one I outlined for the Macintosh.

Fire up iTunes with your iPod connected, select Edit > Preferences, click the iPod tab, and click the Contacts tab in the resulting pane. Within this pane you can elect to synchronize all contacts or just certain groups of contacts. For iTunes to synchronize your contacts with the iPod, Outlook must be running.

Removing contacts from your iPod

So you've broken up with your boyfriend, your favorite dry cleaner has gone out of business, or you can't recall who this "Jane" person is? There's no need to pack your iPod with contacts you don't need; you can remove them easily. Here's how:

1. If your iPod's not connected to your computer, make the connection, and wait for its icon to appear on the Mac's Desktop or in Windows' My Computer window.

2. Configure your iPod so that it mounts on the computer as an external hard drive.

3. Double-click the iPod icon to open the iPod's hard drive.

4. Locate and open the Contacts folder on this hard drive.

5. Select the contacts you'd like to remove, and drag them to the Trash on the Mac or the Recycle Bin on the PC.

6. Disconnect your iPod by dragging its icon to the Trash on the Mac or by unmounting it in Windows' system tray.

tip On a Mac, if the contact you want to remove is part of a single vCard file that contains multiple names, you can edit the contact out in a text editor. Just open the vCard file in a text editor; then delete the BEGIN:vCard and END:vCard entries (and everything in between). The contact will be gone. (Outlook doesn't support vCards that hold multiple contacts.)

Make a Date

As I explained earlier in the chapter, contacts and the iPod carry on their cozy relationship thanks to the vCard standard. Another couple of standards, called the *vCal and iCalendar standards*, help the iPod understand calendar events. These are universal formats for exchanging calendar and scheduling information between vCal- and iCalendar-aware applications and devices.

When you add a calendar event to your iPod, the following information will appear in the Event screen:

• **THE DATE OF THE APPOINTMENT.** Displayed in day/month/year format—11 Jan 2006, for example.

- **THE TIME AND DURATION OF THE APPOINTMENT.**
  Displayed as 4:00–5:30 PM, for example.

- **THE NAME OF THE APPOINTMENT.** If you've named
  it My Appointment in your computer's calendar
  application, so shall it be named on your iPod.

- **THE ATTENDEES.** If you've added attendees to the
  appointment in your computer's calendar application, those names will appear next in the Event
  screen.

- **NOTES.** Any notes you've entered on your
  computer will appear last in the Event screen.

 Visual and audible alarms are also transferred to your
iPod. But you'll see no indication in the Event screen—
or anywhere else, for that matter—that such alarms
exist (though you'll have a pretty good idea when the
alarm goes off).

Working with calendars

Apple would have looked mighty foolish adding
calendaring capabilities to the iPod without also
providing Mac users a calendar application. It did so
by releasing iCal, a free, basic calendar application
that runs under Mac OS X 10.2 and later.

If you have a Mac that's incapable of running the
last couple of iterations of Mac OS X, fear not; iCal
isn't the only Macintosh application that's compatible with the iPod. Both Microsoft Entourage (part
of Microsoft Office X and Microsoft Office 2004 for
Macintosh) and Palm's Palm Desktop 4.x can also
export iPod-compatible vCal files.

Windows users can create iPod-friendly calendar files, too; unfortunately, they can't do it with an Apple application. Although iCal and the Windows iPod were announced in nearly the same breath, Apple didn't feel compelled to release a version of iCal for Windows. Fortunately, Windows users who have a copy of Microsoft Office will discover that Outlook can export calendar files that are compatible with the iPod, as can Palm's Palm Desktop 4.x.

The following sections show you how to make the most of calendars with your computer's common calendar applications.

iCal (Mac OS X 10.2 or later)

Although you can move iCal calendars into your iPod by selecting a calendar in iCal, choosing File > Export, and dragging the resulting calendar file into the iPod's Calendars folder, why bother when iTunes provides a more expedient method? To use iTunes, just follow these steps:

1. Plug your iPod into your Mac.

2. Choose iTunes > Preferences, click the iPod entry, and then click the Calendars tab.

3. Enable the Synchronize iCal Calendars option.

   This is sounding familiar, right? Yes, it's very much like moving contacts via iTunes. Similarly, you can choose to Synchronize All Calendars or Synchronize Selected Calendars Only (**FIGURE 5.3**). When you choose the latter option, just check the boxes next to the calendars you want to copy to the iPod, and click OK.

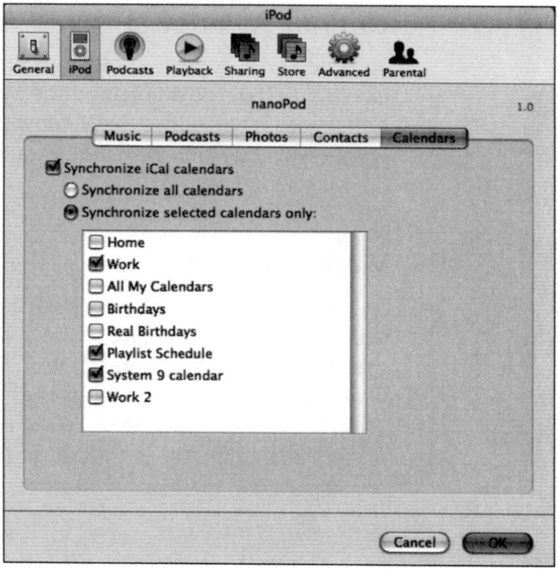

Figure 5.3 The
Calendars
pane in the
Macintosh
version of iTunes

iPod

General iPod Podcasts Playback Sharing Store Advanced Parental

nanoPod   1.0

Music   Podcasts   Photos   Contacts   **Calendars**

☑ Synchronize iCal calendars
   ○ Synchronize all calendars
   ● Synchronize selected calendars only:

   ☐ Home
   ☑ Work
   ☐ All My Calendars
   ☐ Birthdays
   ☐ Real Birthdays
   ☑ Playlist Schedule
   ☑ System 9 calendar
   ☐ Work 2

                                    Cancel   OK

4. Choose File > Update *nameofipod* (where
nameofipod is your iPod's name).

iTunes will synchronize the selected calendars
between your Mac and the iPod.

note

If you've configured your iPod to be updated manually,
choosing the Update command updates only your
contacts, calendars, and—if iTunes is set to update
them automatically—podcasts. iTunes won't overwrite
the iPod's music library with its contents.

Outlook (Windows)

You guessed it—syncing calendars on a Windows PC is darned similar to doing it on the Mac. The major difference is that iTunes for Windows doesn't allow you to sync your iPod with individual Outlook calendars; it's all or nothing.

Viewing events

To view the appointments for a particular day on your iPod, scroll to the date of the appointment on the iPod's calendar, and press Select. In the next window, a list of appointments for that day appears. Scroll to the appointment you want to view, and press Select again. The details of that appointment are displayed in the iPod's Event screen.

Notes-worthy Feature

If you select Notes from the Extras screen on a Dock-connector iPod (notes aren't supported on earlier iPods or, obviously, the screenless iPod shuffle) and then select the Instructions entry, you'll learn that you can view plain-text notes on your iPod. But there's more to know about Notes than that:

- **Notes are strictly limited to 4 kb (kilobits).** If a note exceeds 4 kb, the excess text is cut off.

- **The iPod can hold up to 1,000 notes.** If the iPod's Notes folder contains more than 1,000 notes, only the first 1,000 notes are displayed. (The first 1,000 are determined by alphabetical order rather than creation date.)

- **NOTES ARE CACHED IN MEMORY.** After you've viewed a note, its contents are stored in a 64 Kb (kilobyte) memory cache. This cache is useful because it allows the iPod to display the note without spinning up the hard drive, thereby extending the battery charge. When the cache overflows (because you've read more than 64 Kb of data into it), the oldest notes are given the boot to make room for the information being copied into the cache.

- **NOTES SUPPORT A VERY BASIC SET OF HTML TAGS** (the Hypertext Markup Language codes used to create Web pages). These tags allow you to create notes that link to other notes or to songs on your iPod.

You may be thinking, "Well, ain't this ducky, Chris, but other than providing a place to store directions to Aunt Vilma's suburban manse or the French translation of 'I'm sorry, but this éclair appears to be stuffed with haddock,' what earthly use are these notes?"

Notes can be linked via the HTML tags I mentioned earlier, which opens a host of possibilities. Museums, for example, can use notes that are linked to one another (and to the iPod's audio tracks) to create audio guides, with notes that link to audio descriptions of paintings in a particular gallery. And real estate agents can offer potential buyers iPod-led tours of new properties.

Creating linked notes isn't rocket science, but regrettably, it's involved enough that I can't describe all its ins and outs in this short guide. If you'd like more details, check out the latest edition of my vastly more detailed *Secrets of the iPod and iTunes,* also from Peachpit Press.

6

Accessories

At one time, nearly everything you needed for a happy iPodding experience came in the box: the iPod; a power adapter; the right cables; a case; a remote control; a Dock; and, of course, the software necessary to make it all work. That's changed. As Apple has lowered the iPod's price while offering models with equal or higher capacities, it's determined to protect its profit by making once-bundled accessories pay-for options.

At the risk of verging into the editorial, I don't think that's such a bad thing. Though it was nice enough to get a "free" case and remote control, I quickly threw them into the iPod Extras box that sits next to my desk and replaced them with accessories that suit my tastes. It bothers me not one bit to take the $100 that I saved from the iPod's previous price and devote that money to the accessories I want.

Looking upon the dearth of accessories bundled with today's iPods as an opportunity rather than a punishment, let's examine the kinds of items that will enhance your iPod.

Getting Down to Cases

If you carry around an unprotected iPod or iPod nano, it won't be long before you notice the effect gravity can have on objects dropped from an inverted shirt pocket—or what a pants-pocketful of loose change and keys can do to an iPod's surface. Your iPod needs the protection a good case can provide. And what will such a case provide?

What to look for

A good case should offer the following features:

- A system for attaching the iPod to your body (a belt clip or strap for the iPod; a case, lanyard, or clip for the iPod nano or iPod shuffle)

- Construction sturdy enough to protect the iPod from scratches

- A place to store a full-size iPod's earbuds

These features are the bare minimum you should expect from your case. Frankly, with a piece of bubble wrap, a clothespin, and a couple of pieces of duct tape, you could construct a case that meets these requirements. Looking beyond the essentials, what else might you look for?

- A way to detach the iPod from your body easily

  At times, you'll want to fiddle with the iPod—adjust the volume, flick on the Hold switch, or use the controls to skip a song. Look for a clip that releases quickly and effortlessly.

- A way to access the controls easily

  A standard iPod or iPod nano case that opens in the front lets you fiddle with the controls. You should also be able to access the Headphone jack—and, ideally, the Dock Connector port and Hold switch—without having to disassemble the case.

- Design sturdy enough to provide your iPod a reasonable chance of survival, should you drop it

- Design that makes a statement

  Let's face it—you dropped a lot of cash on your iPod. The iPod is cool. It deserves a cool case.

On the cases

As this book goes to print, there are exactly one jillion iPod cases, and there's no way I can cover them all in this small book. Rather than recommend countless cases, as I do in *Secrets of the iPod and iTunes*, I'll discuss the case styles you're likely to run across and a few standout examples of each kind.

Hard-shell cases

A variety of iPod cases are designed primarily for protection. Oh, sure, they may be as fashionable as can be, but in addition to having a pretty face, they understand that their mission is to keep your iPod from exploding into a passel of parts should you drop it. Some of these cases can be on the bulky side. Marware's (www.marware.com) $40 SportSuit Convertible Case, for example, offers great protection, and it's good-looking, but it won't easily slip into your inside jacket pocket. Others—such as Contour Designs' (www.contourcase.com) $33 Showcase, Matias' (http://matias.ca) $40 iPod Armor, and Vaja's (www.vajacases.com) $80 iVodDJ—are attractive cases that are a little less bulky but still pack a load of protection.

The iPod shuffle can be encased in a tough case as well. A few companies have released metal cases that surround the shuffle. Look for Griffin Technology's (www.griffintechnology.com) $20 iVault and iKeychain. net's (http://keychainpod.com) $30 iKeychain.

Sports cases

Although you can subject hard-shell cases to a load of abuse, if you intend to expose your iPod to hostile environments—particularly those that are more than a little moist—seek a sports case. Cases such as LiliPod's (www.lilipods.com) $40 LiliPod and $35 LiliPod Mini, OtterBox's (www.otterbox.com) $50 OtterBox for iPod, and Apple's own $29 iPod shuffle Sport Case are, at the very least, moistureproof. The LiliPod and OtterBox cases are waterproof up to about 3 feet.

Soft-shell cases

Despite the classification I've slapped on these things, soft-shell cases can also keep your iPod safe from harm. Of these cases, I'm very keen on Waterfield Designs' (www.sfbags.com) $40 iPod Case (**Figure 6.1**). It's nicely constructed and offers good protection, and I find its black ballistic nylon with colored piping attractive. Waterfield also makes the woman's-clutch-purse-like $35 iPod Gear Pouch and $29 Mini iPod Gear Pouch—larger bags for carrying a slew of iPod gear.

Figure 6.1 Waterfield Designs' iPod Case has all the features you'd look for in an iPod case: padding, easy access to controls and ports, a belt clip, and stylish design.

Skins and sleeves

If all you're looking for is protection from scratches, a skin or sleeve for your iPod may be enough. (It's not enough for me, but then again, I'm the cautious sort.) I don't have any particular skins or sleeves to recommend, so I'll leave it up to you to pick one that lights up your life.

Adaptive Technology

Although the iPod's Headphone jack is labeled with the headphones symbol, that jack can accommodate more than just the iPod's earbuds. The iPod's Headphone jack can send out perfectly clean audio from this port to your computer's sound input port or to a home or car stereo. All you need to perform this feat is the right cable. I'll show you exactly which cables to use and how to string them properly from the iPod or Dock to the device of your choice.

iPod to computer

If you want to record directly from your iPod to your computer's audio port, you need an adapter cable that carries stereo Walkman-style miniplugs on both ends. (You can distinguish a stereo miniplug from the mono variety by the two black bands on the plug. A mono miniplug has just one black band.)

You can find such cables at your local electronics boutique for less than $5 for a 6-foot cable. Higher-quality cables that include better shielding, thicker cable, and gold connectors can cost significantly more.

iPod to home stereo

Take the *personal* out of *personal music player* by attaching your iPod or Dock to your home stereo and subjecting the rest of the household to your musical whims. You need nothing more than a cable that features a stereo miniplug on one end and two mono

RCA plugs on the other. A cheap version of this cable costs less than $5.

Plug the miniplug into the iPod's or Dock's audio jack and the two RCA plugs into an input on your stereo receiver (the AUX input, for example). With this arrangement, you can control the volume not only with your stereo's volume control, but also (if the cable is connected to the Headphone port) with the iPod's scroll wheel.

iPod to two headphones

There may (and I hope there *will*) come a time when you'll want to snuggle up with your snookums and listen to your Special Song played on an iPod. A touch of romance goes out of this ritual, however, when you have to split a pair of earbuds between your li'l sweet potato and you.

To bring the intimacy back to your musical relationship, purchase a stereo line splitter. Such an adapter bears a single stereo male miniplug connector on one end (the end you plug into the iPod) and two stereo female miniplug connectors on the other. Plug a pair of headphones into each female connector, and you're set. BTI (www.batterytech.com) makes a $15 headphone splitter with volume controls for each output.

iPod to car stereo

This one's a bit trickier. A few car stereos include a miniplug jack labeled *CD*. If you have such a jack, you're in luck. Just use a stereo miniplug-to-miniplug cable (like the one I recommend for the iPod-to-computer connection), and you're ready to rock. If you don't have a connector, a technician at a Ye Olde Auto Stereo Shoppe may be able to provide one by tapping into a hidden connector on the back of the car stereo. If taking your car to such a tech sounds like a bother, though, you have two other options: a cassette-player adapter or an FM transmitter.

Cassette-player adapter

If your car has a cassette player, you can use a cassette adapter. This thing looks exactly like an audiocassette, save for the thin cable that trails from the back edge. To use one of these adapters, shove it into your car's cassette player, plug its cable into your iPod, and press the Play buttons on both the iPod and the cassette player. Music should issue from your car's speakers.

These adapters cost less than $20.

FM transmitter

These devices work like radio stations, broadcasting whatever is plugged into them to a nearby FM radio. FM transmitters work in a very limited range. Move them more than a dozen feet from the radio's antenna, and you'll pick up interference. For this reason, most are not ideal for use with a home stereo.

Their effectiveness in an automobile depends on how heavily populated the airwaves around you are and how sensitive your car's antenna is. A strong radio signal will overpower these devices, rendering them ineffective. If you live in an urban area with a plethora of active radio stations (or plan to travel in one routinely), you may want to explore a hard-wired connection or a cassette adapter.

Of these adapters, I particularly like Sonnet Technologies' (www.sonnettech.com) $100 PodFreq (**FIGURE 6.2**). It's not cheap, and it works only with third- and fourth-generation (3G and 4G) iPods and color iPods (but not currently with the iPod nano), but it does what it's supposed to do: puts out a signal strong enough to overpower weaker stations and broadcast effectively up to around 30 feet (making it useful around the house).

Figure 6.2
Sonnet Technologies' PodFreq FM transmitter is both bulky and a little pricey, but it provides a strong signal and good sound.

For less money, try Griffin Technology's $40 iTrip (the one with the LCD display). It doesn't have the range of the PodFreq, but it offers a DX "mono" mode that gives it the extra poop you need for a congested FM dial. Also, in International mode, it can broadcast to stations below 88.1 FM—stations that are off limits to U.S. broadcasters. If your radio supports such frequencies, you've got a clear channel to work with. Note: As this book goes to press, the iTrip (along with a host of other accessories) doesn't work with the iPod nano, as it requires an iPod with a Remote Control connector, which the nano lacks.

Power to the People

Like the heads of government, your iPod needs power to do its job. To bring power to your iPod, consider these accessories.

iPod Power Adapter

Regrettably, Apple includes this adapter only with today's full-size color iPods. Because it's a drag to have to find a computer with an available powered USB port (or FireWire port, if you have the right cable) to charge your iPod, I think an iPod Power Adapter is a necessity. Apple sells both flavors—USB and FireWire—for $29.

PocketDock

If you've upgraded from an older iPod to an iPod with a Dock connector, you may be a bit dismayed to discover that some of your old accessories—specifically, gear with FireWire connectors—don't work with your new iPod because of that iPod's proprietary data/power port.

SendStation (www.sendstation.com) comes to the rescue with its $19 PocketDock FireWire (**Figure 6.3**). This just-a-bit-larger-than-a-quarter doohickey bears a standard female 6-pin FireWire connector on one end and Apple's proprietary male data/power connector on the other. When you want to use your old stuff with your new iPod—an auto charger, for example— just plug the PocketDock into the bottom of the iPod, and string a standard FireWire cable between the PocketDock and a device that bears a standard FireWire port.

Figure 6.3
SendStation's
PocketDock
FireWire

SendStation offers three additional versions of the PocketDock. The $23 PocketDock Combo includes both a FireWire and a USB 2.0 port; the $30 PocketDock with Line Out FireWire includes an audio line-out port along with the FireWire port; and the $30 PocketDock with Line Out USB offers a USB connection rather than FireWire and includes the same line-out port.

World Travel Adapter Kit

The iPod can automatically accommodate the world's two major power standards: 115 and 230 volts. The iPod Power Adapter, however, is designed to work only with the kind of plug used in the country in which the iPod was sold. If you plan to take your iPod globetrotting, you'll need the proper plug adapter. Apple's $39 World Travel Adapter Kit contains adapters that support outlets in North America, Japan, China, the United Kingdom, continental Europe, Korea, Australia, and Hong Kong.

Auto charger

To keep your iPod topped off on the road, you need an auto charger. The device plugs into your car's cigarette lighter or 12-volt receptacle; power is delivered to your iPod through a plug that fits into the iPod's data/power port. There are lots of these chargers on the market. I prefer Griffin Technology's $25 PowerJolt (USB) and PowerPod (FireWire) because they include detachable cables, and the PowerJolt's USB port lets you plug an iPod shuffle directly into it.

Backup batteries

Fat lot of good a power adapter and auto charger do you if you're flying halfway around the world or traipsing through one of the less-welcoming Costa Rican jungles during the latest Eco-Challenge. If you plan to be removed from a ready source of power for a period longer than the typical life of an iPod charge, you need some extra help.

Currently, a few companies offer that help. Among them, BTI sells external batteries that clip onto the various Dock-connector iPods. Offered at a street price of around $80, these rechargeable lithium-ion battery packs piggyback onto the rear of the iPod and supply power for an additional 40-plus hours.

To power your shuffle for an extra 20 hours or so, look at Apple's $29 iPod shuffle External Battery Pack.

The Ears Have It

The iPod's earbuds are perfectly serviceable. But this style of headphone is inherently problematic, because (a) not all ear canals are the same size, so a one-size-fits-all set of earbuds may not fit all, and (b) some people get the heebie-jeebies when items are lodged inside their ears. For these reasons, your list of accessories may include an additional set of headphones. Headphones come in a variety of styles—including earbuds, neckband, open-air, and closed—from such companies as Etymotic, Shure, Sony, Koss, Aiwa, Panasonic, Philips, and Sennheiser.

Earbuds

If you like earbud-style headphones but find those included with the iPod to be uncomfortable (particularly if you have the original earbuds, which many users thought were too big), earbuds are available from a variety of manufacturers. Look for earbuds that fit well, don't require a lot of fiddling to focus (meaning that you don't have to move them around continually to make them sound good), and offer reasonably well-balanced sound.

Neckband headphones

These popular headphones are secured to your head
with wires that drape over the tops of your ears.
Imagine putting on a pair of tight glasses backward,
so that the lenses are on the back of your head, and
you'll get the idea. Neckband headphones are comfortable but easy to dislodge if you tug on the cable. Also,
they don't provide a lot of sound isolation, which
means that sounds from outside tend to filter through.

Open-air headphones

Open-air headphones sit over the ears without
enclosing them completely. When you bought your
portable CD or cassette player, open-air headphones
likely were included in the box. These headphones
are comfortable, but the less-expensive models can
sound thin. Like neckband headphones, they don't
provide much isolation.

Closed headphones

Closed headphones cover your ears completely and
provide a lot of isolation, leaving you undistracted by
outside sounds and those around you undisturbed
by a lot of sound bleeding out of your headphones.
Some closed headphones can be a bit bulky and
uncomfortable, particularly if you wear glasses, so be
sure to try before you buy. And because of their size,
these headphones aren't terribly portable.

Shopping for Headphones

You wouldn't purchase a pair of stereo speakers without listening to them, would you? It's just as important to audition a set of headphones that you intend to spend a lot of time with. When you're auditioning those headphones, keep the following factors in mind:

- **Sound quality.** A good set of headphones provides a nice balance of highs and lows without emphasizing one band of frequencies over another. Listen for a natural sound. If the headphones lack brightness—or if you can't clearly discern low-frequency instruments (such as bass guitar, cello, or kick drum), and hearing your music clearly matters to you—move on. These aren't the headphones for you.

- **Comfort and fit.** If you're an enthusiastic listener, you may wear those headphones for long stretches of time. If they pinch your ears or head, slip out of your ears, or fall off your head, you'll grow tired of them quickly.

- **Size.** If you plan to take your headphones with you, look for a pair that fits easily into a pocket or iPod case.

Miscellanea

And then there are the iPod accessories that defy categorization. If you've done the rest, try these accessories on for size.

iPod microphones

Full-size iPods from the 3G iPod onward can record low-quality audio with the help of specialized add-on microphones. Currently, such mics are made by Belkin and Griffin Technology.

Belkin (www.belkin.com) makes the $30 TuneTalk for iPod, the $50 Voice Recorder for iPod w/ Dock Connector, and the $30 Universal Microphone Adapter. The first two include microphones; the latter lets you plug in any mic that features a miniplug.

The Voice Recorder for iPod also includes a small speaker so that you can listen to your recordings. Griffin's $40 iTalk (**Figure 6.4**) has a built-in mic and speaker but also allows you to connect a mic of your own through its miniplug jack. (Griffin's iTalk 2, which features a one-touch recording button, should be out by the time you read this book.)

Figure 6.4
Griffin Technology's iTalk 2 iPod microphone for full-size Dock-connector iPods

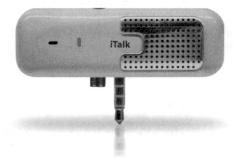

note The iPod can record at only 8 kHz, which is considered to be "voice quality." Although these things are fine for lectures and dictation, you won't use one to bootleg the next concert you attend.

iPod camera connectors

By now, you know that you can add pictures to your color iPod via iTunes. A couple of devices also allow you to import pictures directly to a full-size color iPod (but not an iPod nano). One is Apple's $29 iPod Camera Connector, and another is Belkin's $50 Media Reader for iPod w/ Dock Connector.

The Apple connector plugs into the bottom of your color iPod and features a USB port, which you plug your digital camera cable into. Select the Import command that appears on your iPod's screen when you plug in a camera, and push the Select button. Pictures are downloaded from the camera to your iPod, where they can be viewed immediately (unless they're RAW images—the iPod can't display such images). This connector works only with full-size color iPods.

The Belkin device operates a bit differently. Instead of plugging the camera into the adapter, you remove the camera's media card and plug it into the adapter. Then you follow the usual steps to import pictures to a color iPod, where they can be viewed immediately (again, no RAW images will be displayed). In addition, you can use the Media Reader to store pictures (but not view them) on any full-size Dock-connector iPod.

iPod Remote

If you spend a lot of time with your iPod in inhospitable climates, you may prefer to keep your iPod in your pocket. In that case, you may be a candidate for Apple's iPod Remote. This $39 wired device jacks into your iPod's Headphone and Remote Control ports, and lets you access the iPod's play controls without removing the device from a case or pocket. The iPod Remote includes a set of Apple's earbuds. This accessory is not compatible with the iPod nano.

note
The iPod Remote works only with music; its Forward and Back buttons have no effect on an iPod photo's slideshows. To move through a slideshow, you must use the iPod photo's click wheel.

Another option along these lines is Nyko's (www. nyko.com) $30 iTop Button Relocator, a doodad that fits on top of your Dock-connector iPod to place the iPod's controls and a Headphone port along the top of the device. This is another accessory that's incompatible with the nano.

Wireless remote controls

You can also control your full-size iPod and iPod mini without the benefit of wires via remote controls made by ABT (www.abtech2.com), DLO (www.dlodirect. com), Engineered Audio (www.engineeredaudio. com), Griffin Technology, and TEN Technology (www. tentechnology.com). These are either IR (infrared) or RF (radio frequency) remotes that allow you to control an iPod from a distance, presumably when it's connected to your home or car stereo. The RF remotes—including ABT's $60 iJet and Griffin's $40 AirClick—allow you to stand farther away from the iPod and can work through walls (IR remotes require line-of-sight).

Dock

If you have a full-size iPod or iPod mini, and you routinely plant it next to your computer or home stereo, Apple's $39 Dock is for you. A Dock is particularly useful for those with full-size color iPods, as the Dock includes an S-Video port that allows you to project higher-quality slideshows on an attached television or projector. I'm not sure, however, that Apple's iPod shuffle Dock is worth the dough. It's essentially a USB extension cable in Dock form and, at $29, an expensive one at that.

iPod AV Cable

This is another "Apple used to include it" cable—one that lets you connect your full-size color iPod to a television or projector. The $19 cable features a special miniplug on one end that plugs into the iPod's Headphone jack; the split cable on the other end includes left and right RCA plugs and a composite video connector for plugging into your TV. Because the iPod nano can't project video to televisions, nano owners can skip this one.

iPod speakers

The best way to share your iPod's music with those around you is to jack it into a set of powered speakers. Thanks to the iPod's phenomenal popularity, you can find iPod-friendly speakers that fit just about every budget and taste.

Generally speaking, these speakers include some variety of Dock connector for plugging in your iPod—though many also include a miniplug input port that allows you to plug in older iPods that don't have a Dock Connector port, as well as other audio devices, such as minidisc players and other portable music players.

Altec Lansing's (www.alteclansing.com) inMotion series is a good place to start if you're looking for particularly portable iPod speakers. The $180 iM3 and $100 iM4 speakers are very easy to carry, folding up to the size of a large paperback book.

JBL's (www.jbl.com) On Stage and On Tour speakers ($160 and $100, respectively) are not quite as portable as the inMotion speakers, but they look cool and sound pretty good.

Purists will fight over Tivoli Audio's (www.tivoliaudio.com) $130 Audio iPAL, a great-sounding monophonic AM/FM radio that happens to include an audio input port you can use to connect the iPAL to your iPod's Headphone port. Although said purists will scoff at the idea of using a stereo iPod with a device that broadcasts in mono, they may reluctantly admit that to get the best listening experience from a stereo system, you must plant your ears equidistant from the left and right speakers; this triangulation scheme provides optimal separation between the two stereo speakers. Essentially, this means placing your nose on the front of the inMotion and On Stage speakers.

Better-sounding still is Bose's (www.bose.com) $300 SoundDock (**Figure 6.5**). Featuring great sound in a single package, the SoundDock places the iPod in a Dock slot with a full-face metal grill behind. This grill hides two speakers that are a bit larger than those in the inMotion and On Stage. These larger speakers allow the SoundDock to deliver a richer bass than these other portable systems.

Figure 6.5 Bose's SoundDock

For bigger, better, and even more expensive speakers, check out Klipsch's (www.klipsch.com) $400 iFi. And when I say *bigger,* I mean *Bigger.* This two-satellites-and-subwoofer system is a home stereo system rather than something you're going to take to the beach. The subwoofer is massive, and the satellites are no pipsqueaks.

7

Tips and Tricks

You're far enough along in this little guide to understand that the iPod and iTunes hold more secrets than
just Rip, Click, and Play. This dynamic duo has other
wonders to behold if you know how to unleash them.
And that's exactly the point of this chapter—to shed
light on the lesser-known marvels of the iPod and
iTunes.

Let the magic begin.

Moving Music off the iPod

To deter music piracy, iTunes and the iPod were designed so that music would travel in one direction only: from the computer to the iPod. When you double-click an iPod mounted on a computer, you'll find no folder within that holds the device's music. Yet the music has to be there somewhere.

It is. It's invisible.

When Apple designed the iPod's copy-protection scheme, it did so understanding one of the fundamental laws of this new millennium: That which can be locked will be unlocked (by a 12-year-old boy).

Rather than dump millions of dollars into a complicated copy-protection scheme—which would almost immediately be broken by one of these wily 12-year-olds—the company did the wise thing and protected the iPod in such a way that honest folks wouldn't be tempted to pilfer music off another's iPod. The company's engineers did so by doing nothing more than making the iPod's Music folder invisible. Therefore, the trick to getting the music off the iPod is accessing this invisible folder.

Brute-force techniques

Though fairly graceless, one of the easiest ways to recover your music from an iPod is to make the iPod's Music folder visible and drag it over to your computer's desktop. Then simply add that folder (and the music within) to iTunes by dragging the folder into iTunes' main window or by choosing File > Add to Library in

iTunes. Here's how to do this on either
a Mac or a Windows PC.

Macintosh

The Mac doesn't include a utility for making invisible
files visible, so you must download one. My favorite
tool for this job is Marcel Bresink's free TinkerTool
(www.bresink.de/osx/TinkerTool.html). After you've
downloaded TinkerTool, follow these steps:

1. Plug in the iPod.

2. If iTunes doesn't launch automatically, launch it.

   If the music library on your iPod is not linked to
   iTunes' music library (as would be the case when
   you're restoring your music library from your iPod
   to a fresh copy of iTunes installed on a reformatted
   drive), iTunes will ask if you'd like to replace the
   contents of the iPod with the contents of the
   iTunes Library. Answer No.

3. Select the iPod in iTunes' Source list, and click the
   icon of the iPod that appears at the bottom of
   the iTunes window.

4. Enable the Manually Manage Songs and Playlists
   option, as well as the Enable Disk Use option (these
   options are in iTunes' Music pane); then click OK
   to dismiss the iPod Preferences window.

5. Launch TinkerTool, and click the Finder tab.

6. Enable the Show Hidden and System Files option.

7. Click Relaunch Finder.

8. Move to the Finder, and double-click the iPod's icon on the Desktop.

You'll discover that several more items now appear in the iPod window. Among them is a folder called iPod_Control (**FIGURE 7.1**).

Figure 7.1 The once-invisible iPod_Control folder

iPod_Control

9. Double-click the iPod_Control folder.

Inside the iPod_Control folder, you'll find the Device, iTunes, and Music folders, along with the iPodPrefs file.

10. Drag the Music folder to your Mac's Desktop to copy it to your computer.

As the name implies, this is where music is stored on the iPod.

11. Return to iTunes, and drag the Music folder you just copied to iTunes' main window.

The songs you copied from the iPod are added to iTunes.

tip

If you're a tidy type, before copying those files to iTunes, open iTunes' Preferences window, click the Advanced pane, and make sure the Keep iTunes Music Folder Organized and Copy Files to iTunes Music Folder When Adding to Library options are enabled. Enabling these options will organize your iTunes library in the way that iTunes prefers.

Windows

At the risk of making my Windows readers feel like second-class citizens, please follow the first four steps outlined in the instructions for Mac users. After you've done that:

1. Double-click the My Computer icon on the desktop.

2. Locate your iPod in the window that appears, and select it.

3. Choose Tools > Folder Options in the My Computer window.

4. In the Folder Options window that appears, click the View tab.

5. Below the Hidden Files and Folders entry, enable the Show Hidden Files and Folders option (**Figure 7.2**), and click Apply to reveal the hidden files.

Figure 7.2
Enable the Show Hidden Files and Folders option to view the invisible iPod_Control folder on your Windows PC.

6. Dismiss the Folder Options windows by clicking the OK button.

7. Double-click the iPod's icon in the My Computer window.

8. Sorry about the return to second-class citizen status, but please follow steps 8 through 11 in the Macintosh instructions to complete the process.

More-refined methods

Scan sites such as hotfiles.com and versiontracker. com, and you'll discover a host of utilities designed to pull music off your iPod and onto your computer.

Some of these utilities are more sophisticated than others, allowing you to copy not only the music the iPod carries, but its playlists as well. Here are a few of my favorites.

Macintosh

Whitney Young's free Senuti (http://wbyoung. ambitiouslemon.com/senuti) offers a straightforward interface for moving music off your iPod (**Figure 7.3**). Like similar utilities, it allows you to select songs on the iPod and then copy them to a location of your choosing. Unlike other utilities, Senuti lets you copy not only single songs and songs grouped by artist and album, but also complete playlists from the iPod.

Figure 7.3
Senuti's iTunes-like interface

The Little App Factory's $15 iPodRip (www. thelittleappfactory.com) is another good utility. Like Senuti, it lets you recover songs, albums, and playlists from your iPod to iTunes. It also supports all song information that's stored by iTunes, including ratings, play count, and last played. iPodRip features an iTunes-like interface for easy operation. You can find a version for Windows here as well.

Windows

Unlike other utilities designed to copy music from an iPod to a computer, Jeffrey Harris' free, open-source SharePod (http://sturm.t35.com/sharepod) must be installed on the iPod rather than a host computer. Like other tools, it can extract music from the iPod either as individual files or by playlist. It can also copy the iPod's On-The-Go playlists. And the program lets you create Winamp playlists from the music on the iPod, so you can listen to the iPod's music without copying the music files to your PC.

iPodSoft's $15 iPod Agent (www.ipodsoft.com) can also move music from the iPod to your PC, exporting single songs or playlists. It can't, however, export the iPod's On-The-Go playlists.

Getting the Greatest Charge out of Your iPod

No, I'm not being colloquial. I don't intend to tell you how to get the greatest *thrill* out of your iPod, but how to coax the longest play time from a single battery charge.

KEEP IT WARM (BUT NOT TOO WARM). Lithium-ion batteries perform at their best when they're operated at room temperature. If your iPod is cold, warm it up by putting it under your arm (which, with a really chilly iPod, is an invigorating way to wake up in the morning). And keep your iPod out of your car's hot glove compartment.

FLIP ON THE HOLD SWITCH. If you accidentally turn your iPod on while it's in a pocket, purse, or backpack, you'll be disappointed hours later when you discover that its battery has been drained by playing only for itself. An engaged Hold switch will keep this from occurring.

DON'T TOUCH IT. Okay, that's a bit extreme. What I really mean is that every time you press a button, the iPod has to make an additional effort, which drains the battery more quickly.

TURN OFF EQ AND SOUND CHECK, AND DON'T USE BACKLIGHTING. These extras—particularly back-lighting—eat into your battery's charge.

LOAD YOUR IPOD WITH SONGS SMALLER THAN 9 MB (IPODS WITH HARD DRIVES ONLY). The more often your iPod's hard drive spins up, the more quickly its battery is drained. Files that exceed 9 MB force more frequent hard-drive spins. For this reason, you'll get more play time from your iPod if your song files are in the compressed AAC and MP3 formats versus the big ol' AIFF, WAV, and Apple Lossless formats. Flash-based iPods (the nano and shuffle) don't have hard drives, so feel free to feed them large files.

Shifting Your iTunes Library

It may not happen today, tomorrow, or next year, but if you're a music enthusiast, your computer's startup drive will eventually be so choked with music that you won't have room for anything else. When this happens, you'll want to move your iTunes Library to another hard drive. Here's how:

1. Create a new location for your music files—in a folder on an additional internal or external hard drive, for example.

2. Launch iTunes, and choose iTunes > Preferences (Mac) or Edit > Preferences (Windows) to open the iTunes Preferences window.

3. Click the Advanced pane, and click the Change button.

4. In the resulting Change Music Folder Location dialog box, navigate to the new location you just created, and click Choose.

5. In that same Advanced pane, enable the Keep iTunes Music Folder Organized and Copy Files to iTunes Music Folder When Adding to Library options (**FIGURE 7.4**); then click OK to dismiss the Preferences window.

Figure 7.4
iTunes' Advanced preferences configured for shifting the location of your music library

6. Choose Advanced > Consolidate Library.

As the dialog box that appears indicates, this command will copy all of your music files to the iTunes Music folder—a version of that Music folder that now exists on another drive.

7. Click Consolidate.

iTunes copies not only your tracks to the destination you designated, but also your Library's playlists. (Ratings will be maintained as well.)

Revealing the iPod's Numeric Battery Display

Although the little battery icon in the top-right corner of your iPod's screen is cute, it provides only a very general idea of the iPod's remaining battery charge. Dock-connector iPods (excluding full-size color iPods and the iPod nano) can also display a numeric readout of remaining battery life—from 0 to around 519. To force the iPod to do this, you must plant on it a plain-text file in an invisible folder. Specifically, a file called _show_voltage must appear in the Device folder inside the iPod_Control folder at the root level of the iPod (/iPod_Control/Device/_show_voltage).

To make this trick work, mount your iPod as a removable drive (enable the Enable Disk Use option in the General tab of the iPod Preferences window).

For Mac users

Macintosh users can do this easily by firing up Terminal (located in the Utilities folder inside the Applications folder), entering the text

```
touch /Volumes/iPodname/iPod_Control/
Device/_show_voltage
```

(where **iPodname** is your iPod's name), and pressing Return. Unmount and unplug your iPod, and you'll see the battery charge displayed as a numeric value.

Should you later want to return the battery display to the default graphic image, enter this command in Terminal, and press Return:

```
rm /Volumes/iPodname/iPod_Control/
Device/_show_voltage
```

The Terminal commands should be on a single line, and there should be a space between **touch** and / Volumes and rm and /Volumes.

If your iPod's name includes two or more words separated by a space, you denote those spaces with a backslash (\) and a space. If your iPod's name is Apple iPod, for example, the Terminal entry would read this way:

```
touch /Volumes/Apple\ iPod/iPod_Control/
Device/_show_voltage
```

For Windows users

Create a plain-text file with Notepad or WordPad. When you save that file, be sure that it doesn't include the .txt extension.

Mount the iPod as a removable drive, and open it to the root level. Choose Tools > Folder Options. Click the View tab in the resulting window, and enable the Show Hidden Files and Folders option. Close the Folder Options window.

Navigate this path: YouriPod/iPod_Control/Device. Place the _show_voltage file you created inside the Device folder. Unmount and unplug your iPod, and you'll see the battery charge displayed as a numeric value.

Switch off the Show Hidden Files and Folders option if you don't care to see what's intended to remain hidden.

To restore your iPod's graphic display, follow these same steps, and recycle the _show_voltage file.

 Both the graphic and numeric displays are approximations of the iPod's battery charge. The iPod does its best to guess how much charge it can provide based on current conditions.

The Bootable iPod

Hypnotize your iPod; ask it to travel back, back, *back* to its infancy; and it will murmur that long before it learned to carry a tune, it was little more than a removable hard drive. This capability remains, and if you're a Mac user, this is a feature that you can work to your advantage.

Full-size iPods (sorry, no shuffles, iPod minis, or iPod nanos) can be configured to boot a Macintosh. Better yet, they can be configured thus with very little fuss and bother.

Simply attach the iPod to your Mac via a FireWire cable, insert your Mac OS X installer disc, launch the installer, restart your Mac when requested to do so, designate the iPod as the destination for the OS X installation, and install the OS as you normally would. When the installation is complete, you can choose your iPod as the startup disk within the Startup Disk system preferences and boot from it.

 This process goes smoothly with Mac OS X 10.3 (Panther) and 10.4 (Tiger). OS X 10.2, however, won't install completely from the installer. Instead, you need to clone a bootable volume to the iPod, using a tool such as Carbon Copy Cloner. Don't know what I'm talking about? Upgrade your version of Mac OS to an iPod-friendlier format, or don't bother doing this.

And why would you want to create a bootable iPod? The truth is, you may not need to. You may own the one Macintosh in the world that will never, ever suffer from hard-disk corruption and buggy software. For you, having a reliable bootup disk that contains all your troubleshooting utilities isn't necessary.

Or your musical cravings may be so intense that if you can't cram in every minute of the 41.66 days of continuous music that the 60 GB iPod is capable of storing, you'll wind up with a bad case of the heebie-jeebies (or, worse yet, the jim-jams).

I'm not one of these people. Because I troubleshoot Macs for a living, I find the ability to store all the tools I need on such a portable, bootable hard drive to be a real benefit. And although I love music, I hardly find it limiting to store only a few hundred hours of music on my iPod. It's so easy to replace songs on the device with new material that when I get bored with my current selections, I plug the iPod into my computer and dump a different hundred hours of music onto it. My listening needs are met for the next couple of months.

Even if you don't boot from the iPod, there are good reasons to use a portion of it for data storage. When I hit the road, for example, I drop copies of important documents and presentation on my iPod. That way, should my laptop go south, I've still got the files I need to get my work done. An iPod is also a great sneak-ernet storage device—a handy removable hard drive you can use to transfer large documents from one computer to another when you don't have the ability (or patience) to set up a network.

Spread the Word

If you want to alert your pals to your new favorite podcast, there's no need to send them to the iTunes Music Store. Just select Podcasts in iTunes' Source list, choose the show title you want to share with your friends, and drag it to your computer's desktop. The title will be turned into a podcast subscription file (with a .pcast extension). Email this file to your nearest and dearest. When they drag the file into iTunes (or double-click it), they'll be subscribed to the podcast that's linked to the file.

iPod shuffle, Autofill, Podcasts, and You

iTunes does its best to cram the most music it can onto an iPod shuffle. For this reason, a shuffle won't play AIFF files, which tend to take up a lot of space. Likewise, the Autofill feature that's available when you plug in an iPod shuffle won't add audiobooks or podcasts (which can also be meaty) to a shuffle, even if you've gathered those podcasts into a playlist.

You can, of course, add those files to the shuffle by dragging them to the shuffle entry in iTunes' Source list. Alternatively, if you convert podcasts to a different format—AAC, for example—Autofill will have no objection to pulling them over to the iPod automatically.

To perform that conversion, choose the encoder you'd like to use in the Importing pane of iTunes' Preferences window; then choose Advanced > Convert Selection to XXX (where XXX is the encoder you've chosen in the Importing pane). With the right configuration—the AAC encoder, using the Podcast setting from the Setting pop-up menu, for example—you can create files smaller than the original.

Note that when you convert these files, they'll lose any chapter marks they had, and the podcasts will no longer be bookmarkable. To make a podcast bookmarkable with iTunes 5, select it, choose File > Get Info, click the Options tab, enable the Remember Playback Position option, and click OK.

Adding Radio Stations to iTunes

Select the Radio entry in iTunes' Source list, and if your computer is connected to the Internet, you'll discover that you can listen to streaming Internet radio broadcasts in just about every musical style imaginable. From all appearances, only Apple can add stations to these radio listings. But appearances can be deceiving. You can add other stations to the iTunes Library and to playlists of your own.

To do so, find a station you want streamed to your computer. The free Shoutcast (www.shoutcast.com) provides a load of links to streaming stations. Click the link to the station, and download the resulting .pls (playlist) file to your computer. If the playlist doesn't open in iTunes automatically, drag the file into iTunes' main window; it will appear in the iTunes Library as an MPEG audio stream, which you can listen to (**Figure 7.5**). Now you can create a new playlist and drag your stations into it, thus giving yourself access to all your custom stations from one location.

Figure 7.5
Streaming Internet radio stations in iTunes

Name	Time	Kind
☑ 📶 (#2 – 58/100) KCEA–FM Bi…	Continuous	MPEG audio stream
☑ 📶 (#2 – 444/17809) CLUB 97…	Continuous	MPEG audio stream
☑ 📶 (#3 – 7/10) KCEA–FM Big B…	Continuous	MPEG audio stream
☑ 📶 (#3 – 499/18842) CLUB 97…	Continuous	MPEG audio stream
☑ 📶 (#4 – 11/12) KCEA–FM Big …	Continuous	MPEG audio stream
☑ 📶 (#4 – 1711/18586) CLUB 9…	Continuous	MPEG audio stream
☑ 📶 (#5 – 10/10) CLUB 977 The …	Continuous	MPEG audio stream
☑ 📶 CLUB 977 The 80s Channel	Continuous	MPEG audio stream
☑ 📶 CLUB 977 The Hitz Channel …	Continuous	MPEG audio stream
☑ 📶 KCEA–FM Big Band Swing	Continuous	MPEG audio stream
☑ 📶 TSFJAZZ [www.tsfjazz.com] …	Continuous	MPEG audio stream
☑ 📶 Drone Zone: Atmospheric a…	Continuous	Playlist URL

Making Allowances

If you're like a lot of iTunes Music Store customers, you occasionally bust your budget and purchase more music than you should. To help you keep your spending in check, let me show you how to give yourself an iTunes allowance.

As I mentioned in Chapter 4, the iTunes Music Store allows you to give other users a music allowance—in amounts between $10 and $200—that renews automatically each month. Regrettably, Apple forbids you to create an allowance for the account you've logged in with.

The trick, therefore, is to create an additional Apple ID that supplies an allowance to your original ID. It works this way:

Launch iTunes, and travel to the iTunes Music Store via the Music Store link. If you're signed into The Store, click your ID in the Account field in the top-right corner of the iTunes window. In the resulting Sign In window, click Sign Out. Then click Sign In in the Account field, and in the Sign In window that appears, click Create New Account.

In the window that appears next, agree to the license agreement (if you don't, everything stops here), and create a new account on the Step 2 of 3 page. To do so, you need an email address other than the one you used to create your original Apple ID; Apple tracks its users by email address. On the next page, enter your credit-card information, and complete the process.

note You can create up to five Apple IDs with a single credit-card number. Your request to create a sixth account tied to a particular credit-card account will be denied.

After you've signed in with the new account, click the Allowance link on The Store's main page. Navigate through the allowance-creation screens, and enter your original Apple ID as the recipient of the allowance. You'll have the option to start an allowance right now or to have the allowance kick in at the beginning of the next month.

The last step, of course, requires a measure of self-control. When you've used up your monthly allowance, *stop buying music!*

8

Troubleshooting Your iPod

I regret to report that—except for you, dear reader, and me—nothing is perfect. No, not even the iPod. Whereas it may tick happily along one day, the next day, its menu structure is a mess; it refuses to start up when you're sure it has a full battery; or when it does start up, it displays an icon indicating that it is feeling far from well.

In this chapter, I'll look at the common maladies that afflict the iPod and what, if anything, you can do about them. I'll also examine the hidden diagnostic screen on click-wheel iPods.

Problems and Solutions

Unlike a computer, which can fail in seemingly count-less and creative ways, the iPod exhibits only a few behaviors when it's feeling poorly. Following are the most common problems and (when available) their solutions.

The missing iPod

When you plug your iPod into your Mac or PC, it should make its presence known in short order—appearing in iTunes or some third-party software on your Windows PC. If you've configured your iPod to mount as a disk drive, it will also materialize on the Mac's Desktop or within Windows' My Computer window.

If your iPod formatted for the Macintosh refuses to mount, restart your Mac while holding down the Shift key. This boots your Mac running Mac OS X into Safe Mode. iPods that do not mount otherwise have been known to do so on a Mac running in Safe Mode.

If that doesn't do the trick—or if this trick isn't appli-cable because you're using your iPod with a Windows PC—first reset the first-, second-, or third-generation (1G, 2G, or 3G) iPod by plugging it into a power outlet and holding down the Play and Menu buttons for 6 seconds. If you have a click-wheel iPod, press and hold Select and Menu for 6 seconds. When you see the Apple logo, hold down the Previous and Next buttons on the first three generations of the white iPod, or hold down Select and Play on the click-wheel iPods. This forces the iPod into Disk Mode—a mode that may allow your iPod to mount.

Obviously, neither technique is a good long-term solution, as you don't want to restart your Mac in Safe Mode every time you try to access your iPod or have to force your Mac or Windows iPod into Disk Mode whenever you plug it in. An iPod that won't mount is one that should be restored with the latest iPod Software Updater. On the Mac, boot into Safe Mode; restore the iPod with the Updater (it erases all data on the iPod, so be sure that your data and music are backed up); and restart your computer normally, without holding down the Shift key. With luck, the iPod will appear as expected.

If an iPod formatted for Windows refuses to mount on your Windows PC, and you're using a FireWire card, make sure that the FireWire (IEEE 1394) card is certified by Windows Hardware Quality Labs (WHQL). The literature that came with the card should indicate whether it's compliant; if not, check the vendor's Web site for compatibility information.

PC laptops may not recognize a connected iPod if the computer is configured to turn off power to the USB ports to conserve power. To prevent this from happening, choose Start > Control Panel, double-click the System icon, click the Hardware tab, and click the Device Manager button. In the resulting window, locate the Universal Serial Bus entry in the list of devices, and click the plus sign (+) next to the entry to expand it. Double-click each USB Root Hub entry, click the Power Management tab *(phew, almost finished...)*, disable the Allow the Computer to Turn off This Device to Save Power option, click OK to dismiss the window, and restart the computer.

The confused iPod

Clues that your iPod is confused are the absence of playlists, artists, and songs that used to be there; the failure of the iPod to boot beyond the Apple logo; or the appearance of a folder icon with an exclamation point. I'll look at each scenario in the following sections.

Absence of items

While I was attempting to use a standard iPod formatted for the Macintosh with Windows, my PC crashed, and when I unplugged the iPod, its playlists were missing. I could still play music from the iPod through the Songs screen, but things were not right.

In an attempt to restore a sense of sanity to my iPod, I tried these remedies:

1. **RESET THE IPOD** (again, plug the first three generations of the iPod into a power source and then press and hold Play and Menu for 6 seconds; for click-wheel iPods, press and hold Select and Menu).

   Resetting the iPod is similar to pushing the Reset switch on your computer; it forces the iPod to restart and (ideally) get its little house in order. In this case, the iPod remained confused.

2. **RESTORE THE IPOD** (run the latest iPod Software Updater).

   If resetting doesn't work, or if your iPod can't seem to find its operating system (it displays a folder icon with an exclamation point), there's nothing else for it than to restore the iPod to its original factory state—meaning that all the data on it is removed, and the iPod's firmware is updated. To restore the iPod on the Macintosh, launch the most recent copy of the iPod Software Updater, and click the Restore button in the resulting window (**FIGURE 8.1**). Confirm that you want to restore by clicking Restore in the warning sheet (Mac OS X) that appears.

Figure 8.1 The iPod Software Updater

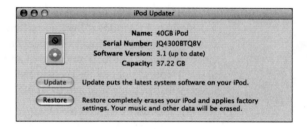

If your iPod is connected via FireWire, it will reboot, and the firmware will be updated. Most click-wheel iPods attached to the computer's USB port will ask to be plugged into a power source, where the update will complete. The iPod nano doesn't ask to be connected to a power source—it will update while plugged into a USB port.

note   This is for your iPod's safety. When the iPod's firmware is being updated—basically, a fresh set of instructions is programmed into a chip inside the iPod—you don't want the iPod to run out of power. If it does, the information written to that chip may be corrupted, making it difficult (perhaps even impossible) to restore your iPod properly.

The procedure is similar on a Windows PC. Use the Start menu to navigate to the iPod folder inside the Program Files folder. Launch the Updater application, located inside the iPod folder. Then click the Restore button to begin the restoration process. Again, if the iPod is connected to a powered FireWire port, it will update without asking you to plug it into a power source.

When you double-click your iPod's icon on the Mac's Desktop or in Windows' My Computer window after the restore, you'll see that the device contains only the Calendars, Contacts, and (on 3G and click-wheel iPods) Notes folders, with the sample contacts and Notes instructions supplied by Apple.

To put your songs back on the iPod, just launch iTunes or the iPod software you use with your Windows PC, and sync the iPod.

Failure to boot

There are a few possible reasons why an iPod might not boot beyond the Apple logo—some benign and others not so.

THE HOLD SWITCH IS ON. Go ahead and smack yourself in the head (and then breathe a sigh of relief) if your iPod won't start up because the Hold switch is engaged.

DRAINED BATTERY. Among the most benign problems is an iPod battery that's drained (though not dead; I'll discuss dead iPod batteries in the "Assault on Batteries" sidebar later in this chapter). If the iPod is functioning normally otherwise, when you attempt to switch on an iPod with a very nearly drained battery, you see a low-battery icon. If the battery is completely drained, the iPod is incapable of mustering the energy even to display this icon; the screen remains black, and the drive refuses to spin up. Plug your iPod into the power adapter or your computer, and let it charge. If everything's hunky-dory after that, pat yourself on the back for a job well done.

If you find that your iPod's battery can't seem to hold a charge for more than a day—say, you switch it off with a full charge on Monday, but its battery is drained when you try to use it on Wednesday—see whether a more recent version of the iPod Software Updater is available from www.apple.com/ipod/download. Some early iPod Software Updater versions are notorious for causing iPods to lose their charge quickly.

If you've plugged the iPod's data/power cable into a computer that isn't currently charging it, unplug it. Some people have reported that when the iPod isn't being charged—when it's attached to a sleeping computer, for example—the charge can dissipate quickly.

In some rare cases, the battery may not be drained enough for the iPod to be reset. If you've tried other solutions and failed, unplug the iPod from a power supply for 24 hours; then plug it into a power source and attempt to reset it by holding down the Play and Menu buttons for 6 seconds on the first three generations of the iPod, or by pressing Select and Menu for those same 6 seconds on a click-wheel iPod.

Songs skip

Songs played on the iPod may skip for several reasons, which include:

Large song file. Large song files (long symphonic movements or those endless Grateful Dead jams, for example) don't play particularly well with the 32 MB RAM buffer on iPods that have a hard drive. Such large files race through the RAM buffer, requiring the iPod to access the hard drive more often. This situation can lead to skipping if the iPod is pulling the song almost directly from the hard drive. If possible, reduce the sizes of files by employing greater compression, or chop really long files (such as audiobooks) into pieces.

Damaged file. A damaged song file may skip. If you find that the same song skips every time you play it—and other songs seem to play back with no problem—go back to the source of the song (an audio CD, for example), rip the song again, and replace the copy on the iPod with the newly ripped version.

iPod that needs to be reset. Yes, an iPod that needs to be reset may cause songs to skip. (Refer to "The confused iPod" earlier in this chapter for instructions.)

iPod that needs to be restored. If a reset won't do the trick, make sure that all the data on your iPod is backed up, and restore the iPod with the latest appropriate version of the iPod Software Updater. (Instructions are also in "The confused iPod" earlier in this chapter.)

Unpleasant sound as the hard drive spins up

This symptom appeared in some early releases of the fourth-generation (4G) iPod and a very few color iPods. Typically, iPods with this problem will make noise through the Headphone port whenever the hard drive spins up. Static accompanies the first couple of seconds of songs played after the iPod spins up.

This appears to be a grounding issue that makes itself known only when you've plugged in headphones whose audio connector bears a metal base that comes into contact with the iPod's case. This metal-to-metal contact transmits this sound through your headphones. To troubleshoot the issue, place a small plastic washer on the post of any affected headphones.

The really confused iPod

Your iPod may be so confused that it won't mount on your Mac's Desktop or in Windows' My Computer window and can't be restored. Follow these steps to mount the iPod:

1. Connect a 1G, 2G, or 3G iPod to a built-in FireWire port on your computer (rather than an unpowered FireWire port on a PC Card or a USB 2.0 port, for example). Because the click-wheel iPods can be powered via a USB 2.0 connection, feel free to use such a connection with your Mac or Windows PC.

2. Reset the 1G, 2G, or 3G iPod by pressing the Play and Menu buttons for 6 seconds. Reset the click-wheel iPods by holding down Select and Menu for 6 seconds.

3. When you see the Apple logo, press and hold the Previous and Next buttons on the first three generations of the iPod until you see a message that reads "Do not disconnect." On the click-wheel iPods, press Select and Play.

The key combination outlined in step 2 resets the iPod much like pressing the Reset switch on a PC or Mac resets the computer. The second key combination forces the iPod into Disk Mode—a mode that will help your computer recognize and mount the iPod.

With luck, your iPod should appear on the Mac's Desktop or in Windows' My Computer window. Then you should be able to restore it with the iPod Software Updater.

Secret Button Combinations

By pressing the proper combination of buttons on the iPod's face, you can force the device to reset, enter Disk Mode, scan its hard disk for damage, and perform a series of diagnostic tests. Here are those combinations and the wonders they perform:

Reset

First three generations of the white iPod: Plug the iPod into a powered FireWire device (the Apple iPod Power Adapter, an auto adapter, or a built-in FireWire port), and press and hold Play and Menu for 6 seconds.

continues on next page

Click-wheel iPods: Plug the iPod into a powered device (the Apple iPod Power Adapter, an auto adapter, or a built-in FireWire port) or a high-powered USB 2.0 port; then press and hold Select and Menu for 6 seconds.

iPod shuffle: Disconnect the shuffle from your computer, move the toggle switch on the back to the Off position, wait 5 seconds, and switch it back to either the Play in Order or Shuffle position. (Yes, resetting a shuffle is really nothing more than turning it off and on again.)

When you reset your iPod, your data remains intact, but the iPod restores the factory settings. This technique reboots the iPod and is helpful when your iPod is locked up.

Disk Mode

First three generations of the white iPod: Reset the iPod. At the Apple logo, press and hold the Previous and Next buttons.

Click-wheel iPods: Reset the iPod. At the Apple logo, press and hold the Select and Play buttons.

Use this technique when you need to mount your iPod on a Mac with an unpowered FireWire card (a FireWire PC Card in your older PowerBook, for example) or on a PC with a similarly unpowered FireWire or USB 2.0 connection.

Disk scan

First three generations of the white iPod: Reset the iPod. At the Apple logo, press and hold Previous, Next, Select, and Menu. An animated icon of a disk and magnifying glass with a progress bar below it appears.

Click-wheel iPods: These iPods don't offer a button combination to scan the hard drive. Rather, you must access this function through the iPod's Diagnostic screen (which I explain at great length in the "Doing Diagnostics" sidebar later in this chapter).

continues on next page

Use this combination when you want to check the integrity of the iPod's hard drive. This test can take 15 to 20 minutes, so be patient. Be sure to plug your iPod into the power adapter when you perform this test so that the iPod doesn't run out of juice before the scan is complete. If the scan shows no problems, a check mark appears over the disk icon on the first three generations of the white iPod.

Diagnostic Mode

First three generations of the white iPod: Reset the iPod. At the Apple logo, press and hold Previous, Next, and Select.

Click-wheel iPods: Reset the iPod. At the Apple logo, press and hold Select and Previous.

See the "Doing Diagnostics" sidebar later in this chapter for more details.

The frozen iPod

Just like a computer, the iPod can freeze from time to time. To thaw it, attach your iPod to a power source—the power adapter, a powered FireWire port, or a computer's high-powered USB 2.0 port—and, on the first three generations of the iPod, press and hold the Play and Menu buttons for 6 seconds. For click-wheel iPods, press and hold Select and Menu for these same 6 seconds.

Failure to charge

There are several reasons why an iPod might not charge. They include all of the following:

A SLEEPING COMPUTER. The iPod won't charge when it's attached to a sleeping computer. Wake up your computer if you want the iPod to charge.

THE WRONG CABLE. Remember, a USB 2.0 connection carries no power to a 3G iPod (though it does to click-wheel iPods). To charge your 1G, 2G, or 3G iPod on a Windows PC, you must plug your iPod into a powered FireWire port or the iPod's power adapter.

MORE THAN ONE FIREWIRE DEVICE ON THE CHAIN.
Although you can chain multiple FireWire devices, doing so with an iPod isn't such a good idea. To begin with, a FireWire device on the chain before the iPod (a hard drive, for example) may be hogging all the power. Second, there have been reports of iPods that got corrupted when they were left on a chain with other FireWire devices. To be safe rather than sorry, don't put the iPod on a chain. If you must use multiple FireWire devices, purchase a powered FireWire hub (which costs between $45 and $65).

A FROZEN IPOD. An iPod that's frozen won't charge. Reset the iPod with the instructions given in "The confused iPod" earlier in the chapter.

A FAULTY CABLE. Cables break. Try a different data/power cable, just in case yours has gone the way of the dodo.

A FAULTY COMPUTER PORT. It's possible that the FireWire or USB 2.0 port on your computer has given up the ghost. Try charging the iPod from the Apple iPod Power Adapter.

A FUNKY POWER ADAPTER. The Apple iPod Power Adapter could also be bad. Attempt to charge your iPod from your computer.

A FAULTY DATA/POWER PORT ON THE IPOD. This problem is more common on 1G and 2G iPods than it is on current iPods. As you plug and unplug the FireWire cable from the iPod's FireWire port, it's possible to put too much stress on the internal connectors that deliver power to your iPod's FireWire port, breaking the bond between those connectors and your iPod's motherboard.

A DEAD BATTERY. Like all lithium-ion batteries, the iPod's battery is good for 300 to 500 full charges. When you've exhausted those charges, your iPod needs a new battery. See the sidebar "Assault on Batteries" for more details.

BROKEN IPOD. iPods occasionally break. If none of these solutions brings your iPod back from its never-ending slumber, it may need to be replaced. Contact Apple at http://depot.info.apple.com/ipod/index.html.

Assault on Batteries

There's been a great deal of hoopla surrounding the iPod's battery—specifically, how long it should last and why it's so darned difficult to replace. Let's set the record straight.

All iPods carry a lithium-ion (Li-ion) battery. Theoretically, Li-ion batteries, by their very nature, can be fully charged up to 500 times. In actual practice, your iPod's battery will put up with between 300 and 450 complete charges before it gives up the ghost.

This is all well and good if you charge your iPod once a week or so. However, if you use your iPod constantly—and, thus, fully charge it four or five times a week—you'll discover that after about a year and a half, it's kaput.

As you might imagine, those who've seen their iPods kick the bucket after a year and a half have been less than joyous about it. After all, a device you paid several hundred dollars for should have a longer shelf life than a Twinkie. Adding to this unhappiness was Apple's policy of charging $255 to replace the iPod.

Apple and some third-party battery vendors got hip to the situation as the first couple of revisions of the iPod began to go south due to dead batteries.

If your iPod is more than a year old, and it fails to hold a charge, Apple will replace it with another "functionally equivalent new, used, or refurbished iPod" for $59 (plus $6.95 for shipping). That "functionally equivalent" stuff means that you won't get back the same iPod that you send in. You'll get one in the "good pile" that has the same capacity and is of the same generation as the one you sent in. If you send in an engraved iPod, Apple will take the back plate off your iPod and put it on the replacement iPod. For more details, visit http://depot.info.apple.com/ipod/index.html.

iPodResQ (www.ipodresq.com) offers a battery-replacement service for $64. You contact the company, it ships you a postage-paid box for your iPod, you ship it to iPodResQ HQ, and your iPod

continues on next page

is returned in a few days with a brand-new battery. PDASmart (www.pdasmart.com) will do the job for around $60.

If you're a do-it-yourselfer, you can procure a battery and service the iPod on your own. You can get battery-replacement kits from BatteryShip (www.batteryship.com), ipodjuice.com (www.ipodjuice.com), iPodResQ, Other World Computing (http://eshop.macsales.com), PDASmart, Small Dog Electronics (www.smalldog.com), Laptops for Less (www.ipodbattery.com), Unity Electronics (www.unityelectronics.com), and many more outfits. Along with the battery, these companies include tools for opening the iPod and instructions for doing so. Replacement batteries run just under $30.

Note: Each generation of the iPod is increasingly difficult to crack open. The 1G and 2G iPods can be opened by most creatures with opposable thumbs, but there's a real danger of destroying your iPod once you move into 3G-and-later iPods. (Successfully replacing the battery in an iPod mini, for example, is about as easy as removing your own kidney.) Unless you're extremely confident in your ability to tear apart tiny machines, have a professional replace your battery.

The broken iPod

It's a machine, and regrettably, machines break. If none of these solutions brings your iPod back from the dead, it may need to be repaired. If you live near one, take it into an Apple Store or to another outfit that sells iPods. If such a trip is impractical, contact Apple at http://depot.info.apple.com/ipod/index.html for instructions on how to have your iPod serviced.

When you bring a misbehaving iPod to a Genius at the Apple Store, said Genius will run a couple of tests on it. If it fails to respond, he or she may try to restore it (which is why you should always have a backup of your music and data).

If that doesn't work, and your iPod is under warranty, you'll probably get a replacement on the spot (provided that it's an iPod model of the same capacity that Apple is currently selling). If you have an iPod under warranty, and Apple's changed the iPod line—you've got a 30 GB iPod photo, for example, and Apple sells color iPods only in 20 and 60 GB capacities—Apple will arrange to get you an iPod of similar capacity. (Sorry, but you're unlikely to get the next size up, even though it sells for the same price you paid for yours.) If the iPod is out of warranty, you'll have to pay for the repair.

Doing Diagnostics

Ever wonder what Apple technicians do when they want to test an iPod? Just as you can, they reset the iPod, and when they see the Apple logo, they press Previous, Next, and Select on the first three generations of the white iPod, and Select and Previous on click-wheel iPods.

When you do this, you'll hear a chirp. Release the buttons. You'll see (very briefly) a reversed Apple logo and a screen of text that eventually resolves to a list of tests.

In the big ol' *Secrets of the iPod and iTunes,* I detail each of these tests. I don't have the room to do so here, but I can give you the gist.

Most of these tests take a gander at the iPod's controllers and internal components: the hard drive, display, SDRAM chip, battery, and Headphone and Dock Connector ports. For most people,

continues on next page

these tests are nothing more than a curiosity, which is one reason Apple refuses to talk about the Diagnostic screen.

For those with click-wheel iPods, however, these tests can be helpful. Specifically, the tests that scan the hard drive can go a long way toward telling you whether your iPod's hard drive is on the way out. How you access the hard-drive test depends on which iPod model you have.

4G iPod: Reset the iPod by holding Select and Menu for 6 seconds. When you see the Apple logo, press Select and Previous until you see the Apple logo reverse and the iPod blink. When you let go, press Next to scroll down the list of tests until you select HDD Scan. Press Next and Select to begin the test. Be sure that the iPod is plugged into a power source during this test, as it will drain a battery quickly. If your iPod's hard drive is OK, you'll eventually see HDD Pass. And if it's not OK? Beats me—Apple won't talk about it, and I've never had a hard drive fail. My best guess is that if you see something other than HDD Pass, there's a problem that warrants a peek by Apple's techs.

Color iPods and iPod mini: Reset the iPod by holding Select and Menu for 6 seconds. When you see the Apple logo, press Select and Previous until you see the Apple logo reverse and the iPod blink. When the Diagnostic screen appears, press Next until IO is highlighted. Press Select, and click Next until HardDrive is selected. Press Select again, and press Next to select HDScan. Plug the iPod into a power source before running the scan, as it will drain the battery quickly. If the iPod's hard drive is OK, you will be taken back to the HardDrive screen.

iPod nano: This iPod has no hard drive, but you can check its flash memory. Enter Diagnostic Mode as you do with a color iPod or mini, and click the Next button to select FlashScan. If the iPod passes, you'll see Test OK.

To exit Diagnostic Mode, reset the iPod by pressing Select and Menu for 6 seconds.

Thank You

As thanks for purchasing this book, I'd like to give you a little something to put on your iPod. That little something is *Of Eve*, a solo piano album I recorded some years ago.

The music on *Of Eve* belongs to me, but you're welcome to download and place it on your computer and iPod for your personal listening pleasure. You may not, however, use this music in a public broadcast or for any commercial purposes without my permission.

You can find your copy here: www.peachpit.com/ipodsecrets.

I hope you enjoy it.

Index

You've Had a Look, Now Take a Listen!

Reading about the perfect iMix playlists is fun, but actually listening to them is even better, which is why we've made links to the iMixes featured in The iPod Playlist Book available at the Peachpit Web site. Just click on a link to buy the entire playlist from Apple's iTunes Music store. Head to www.peachpit.com/playlistbook and rock out to your favorite iMixes today!

While you're shopping for playlists at the Peachpit site, we invite you to post your comments about each iMix and let us know which songs we left out, which ones should have never made the cut, and why you just can't get enough of Nina Simone, Eminem, Ashlee Simpson, Johnny Cash, The White Stripes, The Clash, or whomever else rocks your world. Blog on today.We want to hear from you!